DARING TO DREAM

Series in Critical Narrative
Edited by Donaldo Macedo
University of Massachusetts Boston

Now in print

The Hegemony of English
  by Donaldo Macedo, Bessie Dendrinos, and
    Panayota Gounari (2003)

Letters from Lexington: Reflections on Propaganda
New Updated Edition
  by Noam Chomsky (2004)

Pedogogy of Indignation
  by Paulo Freire (2004)

Howard Zinn on Democratic Education
  by Howard Zinn, with Donaldo Macedo (2005)

The Globalization of Racism
  Edited by Donaldo Macedo and Panayota Gounari
    (2005)

Daring to Dream: Toward a Pedagogy of the Unfinished
  by Paulo Freire (2007)

Forthcoming in the series

Dear Paulo: Letters from Teachers
  by Sonia Nieto

DARING TO DREAM
TOWARD A PEDAGOGY OF THE UNFINISHED

by

PAULO FREIRE

Organized and Presented by Ana Maria Araújo Freire
Translated by Alexandre K. Oliveira

Paradigm Publishers
Boulder • London

Copyright © 2007 Ana Maria Araújo Freire

Published in the United States by Paradigm Publishers, 3360 Mitchell Lane, Suite E, Boulder, CO 80301 USA.

Paradigm Publishers is the trade name of Birkenkamp & Company, LLC, Dean Birkenkamp, President and Publisher.

Library of Congress Cataloging-in-Publication Data

Freire, Paulo, 1921–1997.
 [Pedagogia dos sonhos possíveis. English]
 Daring to dream : toward a pedagogy of the unfinished / Paulo Freire ; edited by Ana Maria Araújo Freire ; translated by Alexandre K. Oliveira.
   p. cm. — (Series in critical narrative)
 Includes bibliographical references and index.
 ISBN 978-1-59451-052-6 (hardcover : alk. paper)   1. Critical pedagogy.   2. Education—Philosophy.   I. Freire, Ana Maria Araújo, 1933–   II. Title.
 LC196.F74513 2007
 370.11'5—dc22

                                                            2007010260

Printed and bound in the United States of America on acid-free paper that meets the standards of the American National Standard for Permanence of Paper for Printed Library Materials.

Designed and Typeset by Straight Creek Bookmakers.

11 10 09 08 07   1 2 3 4 5

CONTENTS

∽

Contents

INTRODUCTION

✌

Dreaming is not only a necessary political act, but also a connotation of men and women's social-historical form of being. It is part of human nature, which finds itself within history, in a permanent process of becoming.... There is no change without dreams just as there are no dreams without hope....

The understanding of history as *possibility* rather than *determinism* ... would be unintelligible without *dreams,* just as a *deterministic* view feels incompatible with them and, therefore, negates them.

(Paulo Freire, *Pedagogia da esperança,*
1992: 91–92)

The more I might let myself be seduced by the acceptance of the death of history, the more I would admit that the impossibility of a different tomorrow implies an eternity of the neo-liberal today we see now, and the permanence of today kills within me the possibility of dreaming. By deproblematizing time, the so-called death of history decrees immobilism that negates human beings.

> (Paulo Freire, *Pedagogia da autonomia*, 1997: 130)

Risk only makes sense when I run it for a valuable reason, an ideal, a dream beyond risk itself.

> (Paulo Freire, *À sombra desta mangueira*, 2000: 57)

When I think about my Earth, I think above all what is possible but which is never easy—dream of reinventing democracy in our society.

> (Ibid.: 32)

I could never think of educational practice ... as untouched by the issue of values, therefore of ethics, by the issue of dreams and utopia, in other words, of political choices, by the issue of knowledge and beautifulness, that is, of gnosiology and aesthetics.

> (Paulo Freire, *Pedagogia da indignação*, 2000: 89)

Therefore, to the language of possibility, which supports utopia as a *possible dream*, they prefer the neoliberal discourse, one pragmatic and according to which we must adapt to facts as they are taking place, as if they could not unfold in a different manner, as if we did not have to fight, precisely while men and women, so that they can take place in a different manner.

(Paulo Freire, *Pedagogia da esperança,*
1992: 90–91)

The dream for humanization, whose concretization is always process, always becoming, goes through rupture with real, concrete ties of an economic order, a political one, social, ideological, etc., which are dooming us to dehumanization. *Dreaming* is, therefore, a requirement or a condition which has become permanent in the history we make and which makes and re-makes us.

(Ibid.: 99)

It is in commemoration of the date when Paulo would have turned eighty years old—of a life lived as a plentiful and fertile *existence,* as a complex, rich, and profound experience as was his of being *with* others, men and women, *with* the world, one marked as very few by dignity, coherence, and lovingness—that I bring to the public a new book of his writings within the "Paulo Freire Series."[1]

This work is thus the result of my efforts, on the one hand, to satisfy the constant interest of Paulo's readers concerned with liberating education and, on the other hand, to eternalize his way of being *human,* through socializing as much as possible with his always-hopeful words and deeds. His very own brand of *existing* is one profoundly marked by an ethical-political-educational concern for human beings, indistinctly.

I speak of *existence* as Paulo conceived of it, the human experience that opens up to men and women alike to possibilities for speaking and expressing our most elaborate thinking and for manifesting our most genuine emotions in different ways. Thinking and feeling are generated in nondichotomized fashion within our bodies, thus making them into *conscious bodies*. Such is an *existence* that, by its very nature, opens up to us the possibility even to be able to reflect on that existence itself and on our capacity for creating praxis, as we speak, think, act, and for writing about its beautifulness. It is an absolutely humanly peculiar existence, where, while knowing what we want and feel, we are able to transform the world. Paulo's *existence,* his ethical-political-pedagogical *existing,* is thusly identified with *dreaming,* with the *utopia* of a better world, one more just. In this radically ethical existing of his, Paulo offered us a theory that enables us to become conscious of our role as ethical subjects of history and therefore able, if we so wish, through cultural action propelled by *dreams,* to make viable our *liberating utopia.*

It is human *existence,* therefore, that allows for denouncing and announcing, indignation and love, conflict and consensus, dialogue or its negation through the verticality of power. Ethical greatness antagonizes antiethical shortcomings. It is precisely from those contradictions that *collectively envisioned dreaming* is born, and we, all men and women, attain possibilities for overcoming life conditions to which we are subjected as mere objects and becoming *Being More*.[2] Paulo's epistemology convinces and invites us—especially those of us who are educators—to think and choose, to join in and take action in continually projecting the concretization of *possible dreams* whose nature is as ethical as it is political. We must believe that we can make *apparently impossible dreams* possible, so long as we live out that *existing*, truly. It is *dreaming* and *existing* that "allows" us to keep making ourselves into beings who fight for liberation, *Being More*.

Today, as we analyze global circumstances, we can verify, almost without any difficulty, even without being political scientists or economists—the demiurges of globalization!—a hardening of contradictions, one for years denounced by Paulo, that culminates in a state of greater and greater injustice at every level and degree dictated by the globalization of the economy. This postmodern way of controlling the destiny of the world and of all people, that concentrates national incomes in the hands of few people and countries, magnanimously dispenses, in order to maintain itself, a policy of indebtedness, national sovereignty negation, and misery of all sorts. There is hunger and disease, multiple afflictions that more and more render fragile most of the population in Africa, in Latin America, as well as in significant segments within societies of the all-powerful North. We, Brazilian men and women, are, rigorously speaking, as disempowered each day as our fellow Latin Americans, even though less so than our ethnic and cultural origin forefathers, the Africans. We feel and we know ourselves as perversely subtracted as ever in our conditions and possibilities for being, for having, for desiring, for wanting, and for attaining.

The most en vogue news in the Brazilian media nowadays is about corruption-related crimes of all sorts, especially those originating in our political society. Some corrode public coffers or, better yet, the dignity of the Brazilian people, as in those coffers ought to be duly guarded and respected, if those politicians were serious and ethical, the product of our work, arrived at through the sweat if not the blood of our people. Nevertheless, we are stunned to realize that, even when investigated, such politicians end up simply being cited for this or that indication of "forgivable offenses," but not held accountable for the crimes they have in fact committed —and that they shamelessly and callously continue to commit, certain as they are of their privileges. The legal subterfuge employed by the lawyers—who almost always become wealthy exactly for defending the indefensible, in the name of "a citizen's right to defense," with the morose judiciary's looking the other way and attaining itself to the "letter of the law," often out-of-date in terms of the true ethics of our historic times—indeed helps perpetuate impunity for those who have and can do everything. Others find refuge in public service so as to embezzle freely. They lie to their constituents, show contempt for public opinion, kill without mercy on a whim or out of interest, build and sell condemned buildings sure to collapse due to the precariousness of their planning and construction, engage in drug trafficking, and that of young athletes or girls for prostitution, and shamelessly use them to illicitly enrich themselves. These deeply immoral and illegitimate forms of behavior have been contributing, no doubt, to increasing the generalized and unbearable state of criminality in the country.

Other men are piled up in correctional facilities, most of the times for much lesser crimes, as if they had no body or soul, as if they were nothing, in reality like things that must be eliminated either mutually in mutinies or by cruel and unscrupulous professionals, often under orders of authorities that can only see crime in the people filling jailhouses, the ones belonging to the popular segments of society. Citizens no longer trust the police forces and fear them instead. Force members, on their part, denounce and make us see the inhospitable reality in which they work and live due to the absence of a much-needed, serious security policy for the population. Part of this outraged and impotent population must watch all this and become incredulous about life, about other men and women; it ceases to envision possibilities for *existing* fully. Another part takes advantage of the tide and rides it, in the muddy seas of authority abuses, pillaging, and a dog-eat-dog, every-man-for-himself misgovernance, an unabashed usurpation of the rights of others, all of which seem to drown us as ever before, both as a people and as a nation.

Our public wealth, painstakingly built through centuries of history, tenacity, and bravery by a people as creative as it is hardworking, is being handed over with no scruples or abashment to private interests, under directive of the misguided neoliberal notion that the private sector has the ability to provide well for the management of all stages of production and distribution of goods and services, whereas the public sector does not. We verify to our outrage that, from agricultural and agrarian policies—to include those for financing the production of transgenic crops by the future "owners" of all food seeds on the planet and our deficient arable land distribution, the indispensable and urgently needed agrarian reform—to those in the energy sector and other public policies, there is a lack of strategic political vision on the part of our government, "allied and aligned," in reality subjected to the dictums of global power, one evil and necessarily alien to the crucial, dramatic, and current social, economic, financial, and environmental problems of the Brazilian nation.

Proposed solutions born from within social movements and that translate the voice of the people's majority, even if realistically developed on the basis of our concrete economic, social, and historic reality, are treated with disdain, ridiculed, and abandoned by the "owners of power," and they may render their proponents persecuted and accused of engaging in political behavior, as if being a political being, through the exercise of true citizenship were the prerogative of the ruling elite only. The most confounding example is the opposition to the Movement of Landless Rural Workers (MST). Their actions and proposals toward sustainable development on a social-humanist basis lend credibility to the dream of democratizing the country and go beyond the simple "donation" of land to those who occupy it—above all, they want to insert themselves in the country's productive sector and culture as citizens. Their ideas are undermined and the movement's militants meet sanguinary persecution. Their political and civil rights may even get "bruised." In the meanwhile, our cities watch as the destitute die on hospital lines, live on the streets, waste with hunger, and are excluded from schooling.

It is incredible that just two years ago I was certain that, among the many forms of facing up to the world proposed by Paulo, the best one would be indignation,[3] if our intentions were to change the world, to transform it for the better. Today, in light of the absolutely terrifying and despairing situation taking hold of our country, at the likeness of what is going on in other "emerging countries" of the world—a fact that should not ease or make disappear our feelings of repudiation toward the political-economic model that crushes us, but rather heighten them as it proves just what globalization and its defenders are all about. I have come to understand that we must shift the focus of the preparatory reflections to our actions. As I reread almost all of Paulo's body of work, at the same time that I was analyzing and organizing articles for this book, I noticed that, starting from *Pedagogy of Hope*, he had been inviting us, yes, to feel indignation, but also already pointing us toward reaching a strategy—democracy—of gradually overcoming that affective-political stage and envisioning dreams of change. He was already inviting us, and had been making us see the need, to gradually incorporate our ethical and political dreams into indignation and love, as a human necessity, one even more radical when we need to face up, as we do now, to society's difficult problems.

What I mean is that, while still feeling our indignation and love, but also starting out from that very indignation—especially since very little or none of it is being heard by those in power with respect to our clamors—we must nurture dreams, which we can almost always make possible, so that we can continue, in fact, to be and to feel as men and women, as subjects of history. It is about a true *existence*. Lest all indignation drain away completely and disheartening fright or destabilizing absence of hope or adaptive cynicism take hold, I heeded Paulo's "calls," as he was indeed "guessing" or in reality picking up on the signs of the unacceptable situation in the world today and in Brazil in particular; he spoke about and demonstrated the importance of *utopian dreaming* in various essays and talks.

As contradictory as this may seem, we urgently need, therefore, to revive within ourselves our *ontological capacity for dreaming,* for projecting days of peace, equity, and solidarity into the closest possible future. We must reactivate within our conscious bodies the possibilities for dreaming that *utopian* dream Paulo had been inviting us to dream for years—that *possible dream*—the one that allows us to reclaim within ourselves all of our most authentic humanity, of which we have been robbed by those who exploit and mutilate us, and those who mine our hopes for making ours into as serious and as just a society as we deserve.

Therefore, we need to believe, *with* and *like* Paulo, that "part of the turmoil of the soul is also in the pain of a ruptured dream or utopia,"[4] such as he must have felt some time in his life, and such as most of us Brazilians profoundly feel today. Contradictorily, however, from those "torn but not undone dreams,"[5] we can rekindle within ourselves the hope of a new society. Let those of us committed to a better world, and who feel, today more than ever, that our dreams are being "*torn*," seek once again, *in* and *with* Paulo, to socially remake our *possible dreams* of transformation, as we know they have only apparently been "*undone*," since *dreaming* is given fate. That is, we are irreversibly and fortunately "condemned," all men and women who have *existed* and made themselves human beings through millennia, to *dreaming*: to dreaming humanizing dreams, ethical-political dreams. Those *possible dreams* become pedagogical and must be socialized: *Pedagogy of Dreaming*.

The book I present here is made up of various works by Paulo, as always denouncing the suffering of the oppressed, of the persecuted, the exploited, the excluded, of the shirtless of the world, but also announcing as always that we shall not remain impassive and wait in vain. He invites us to *dream*, to dream those *possible dreams* and to act toward making our *dreams possible*. He invites us to make possible the dream of transforming the world into a better more just world.

Each of the two parts making up the book presents four works, previously unpublished for the most part (or not published in Brazil), and they are grouped as "Commentaries and Essays" and "Dialogues and Conferences." I tried to maintain a chronological order in each group of when the pieces were written, except for the first selection. This section was chosen for being the last of Paulo's systematized thinking; it reveals his concern with injustice and solidarity toward those who fight for *possible dreams,* to the last moment of his life. Part I, "Commentaries and Essays," contains the above-mentioned selection retitled "Impossible to Exist without Dreams," which endorses MST militant action and the movement's very reading of the world. "On the Cognitional Act" has tremendous historic value, even if incomplete, as this never-published writing was Paulo's "rehearsal" for what he would soon say in *Pedagogy of the Oppressed* and in a few writings that make up *Cultural Action of Liberation.* (I added the word *women* to his then-sexist text whenever appropriate, since Paulo himself had requested from publishers the same be done for *Pedagogy of Hope.*) The piece is followed by "History as Possibility," from 1993 (we have yet to figure out whether it has been published in Portugal or not), and "A Few Reflections around Utopia." In Part II, "Dialogues and Conferences," readers will find "Human Rights and Liberating Education," from 1988, never put to written form before; "A Conversation with Students," a beautiful dialogue with students at the Escola Vera Cruz, in São Paulo; "Changing Is Difficult, but Possible," a statement-topic Paulo never tired to return to in the final days of his life, always encouraging us toward hope as a utopian life project; and "Dialogue with the Participants: The Reading and Writing Issue."

Finally, I invited a dear friend of mine, Ana Lúcia Souza de Freitas, to write the Foreword. Ana Lúcia produced a beautiful and densely theoretical piece, familiar as she is in her praxis with the issues addressed/proposed in Paulo's understanding of education; she has re-created them in her work settings, both at the City of Porto Alegre Department of Education (SMED/POA) and in her teaching and research in the Possible Dream Project at LaSalle University, Unisalle. Without being idealistic, but due more to her degree of epistemological daring, she asserts herself, without fears or hesitations, as an authentic *dreamer*, thus believing, *with* and *like* Paulo,[6] in the possibility that men and women can do what is possible so that the impossible, or what simply seems that way, becomes *possible dreams*.

Nita
Ana Maria Araújo Freire
São Paulo, August 19, 2001

Postscript: This presentation, so recently written, when *Daring to Dream* had gone to press, may seem dated at first blush, or at least incomplete, after September 11. In light of the fright that gripped all of us, men and women, with the explosion of the World Trade Center and its despairing consequences for the whole world, in light of the restlessness that had already been growing with the development of a "globalized world" that has only been benefiting a few men and women who seek to enrich themselves in every manner, at every level, to every degree, I asked myself, seriously, "Is what I wrote still valid?" What world is this we are building? Are we losing hope for better days or should this attack against life and peace be understood, contradictorily, as the start of a possibility for understanding and for a project for the world where *dialogue on tolerance and diversity* will lead us to a time/space with more harmony, justice, and tranquility?

Stunned within this atmosphere of misunderstanding and terrorism, I reflected at the same time, "Should I, due to the tragic, warring world context today, forget or minimize the dramatic nature of the day-to-day context experienced in Brazil? Should I forget or minimize this situation that has been resulting direr in the past few decades precisely due to the imperialistic purposes that 'justify' such ignominious acts?" Therefore, by way of negating duality, a compartmentalization of problems in insulated, closed departments, as if to say that "what happened there" is a matter of religious fundamentalism or "one of revenge against those who have sown discord," I decided not to change what was already written. Thus, the original presentation remains, but not without an addition, a warning for our reflections: either we will identify with liberating ethics, thus humanistic ethics, with utopias where there is room for differences, purging ourselves and purging the planetary society of discriminations and socializing ourselves into building the possible dreams of tolerance and democracy; or we will march at an accelerated pace toward the self-destruction of human beings.

São Paulo, October 15, 2001

ENDNOTES

1. The Paulo Freire Series was something I proposed, and the Editora UNESP leadership and its executive editor imme-

diately accepted the idea as a commemoration of the eightieth anniversary of Paulo Freire's birth in Recife, on September 19, 1921. The first volume in this collection is *A pedagogia da libertação em Paulo Freire*, org. Ana Maria Araújo Freire, series editor (São Paulo: Editora UNESP, 2001).

2. The expression *Being More* is used here and the subsequent chapters by Paulo Freire to refer to our capacity to expand our humanity. *Being More* should not be interpreted as the accumulation of material wealth or as some form of career ladder.

3. This refers to the book I put together in celebration of Paulo's rewarding existence among us, in May 2000, made up of the last pieces written by him and that I titled, as explained in the book, *Pedagogia da Indignação* (São Paulo: Editora UNESP, 2000).

4. Paulo Freire, *Pedagogia da esperança* (São Paulo: Paz e Terra, 1992), 33.

5. Ibid., 35.

6. "Historical vocation is not fate, but rather possibility. And there is no possibility that is not exposed to its negation, to impossibility. Vice-versa, *what is impossible today may come to be possible some day.*" (Paulo Freire, *À sombra desta mangueira*, 3d ed. [São Paulo: Olho D'Água, 2000], 82, my emphasis.)

FOREWORD

Ana Lúcia Souza de Freitas

⊹

Daring to Dream is, no doubt, a powerful manner to express the *pedagogical strength* Paulo provided us with through his life and work. Paulo Reglus Neves Freire— who would be entering his eightieth year of existence at the start of the new millennium—left us an important legacy that keeps his presence alive in the struggle of those who continue to believe in the possibility that education, in spite of its limits, can *turn the impossible into possible* and who conceive that as a challenge for popular education practice. Paulo Freire bears testimony of that possibility as he engages in a practice founded on a necessary opening toward the other, a practice where dialogue is an epistemological requirement for living that is socially committed, where reflection is collectively shared and generates multiple authoring.

Having referred to himself as *one who treads on the obvious,* Paulo Freire problematizes our very thinking about obviousness, reasoning that "the obvious is not always as obvious as we think it is."[1] The starting point of this understanding will allow me to single out some items of *obviousness* provided by the reading of Paulo Freire, as a result of which we can envision the basis for a pedagogy that orients the daily experience of a *liberating educational praxis: Daring to Dream. Education: The Possible Dream* was the reflection proposed by Paulo Freire to virtually a *multitude* of educators who participated in his first major conference in Brazil after sixteen years in exile.[2] Interested in thinking, "out loud," through some issues that were disquieting him with respect to the understanding of education as an act of knowledge and to its implications for the political nature of educational practice, Freire discussed the place of *possible dreams* within a *liberating concept of education.* With that expression, he demarcated the utopian nature of liberating educational practice, "utopian in the sense that this practice lives the dialectic, dynamic unity between denunciation and annunciation, between denouncing an unjust, exploitative society and announcing the possible dream for one that is, at least, less exploitative."[3]

From that reflection stem certain points that deserve to be emphasized and understood. It is important to say that the *possible dream* is not a matter of some naive idealization; rather, it emerges precisely from critical reflection on the oppressive social conditions, which are not perceived in deterministic fashion, but with an understanding of reality as mutable through the engagement of the subjects who constitute it, as they are equally constituted by it. Therefore, including oneself in the struggle for *possible dreams* implies accepting a double commitment: one with denouncing the excluding reality and with announcing the possibilities for making it democratic. In sum, it is a matter of accepting, as a challenge resulting from liberating pedagogic practice, what Freire termed the *untested feasibility,* a term present ever since his first writings.

In her thorough explicative notes to the book *Pedagogy of Hope,* Ana Maria Araújo Freire emphasizes the importance of understanding untested feasibility in accepting *history as possibility,* in opposition to a fatalistic view of reality. Such perspective, characteristic of critical consciousness, sees history as constituting itself through the confrontation of *limit situations* as they present themselves in social and personal experience, while also considering that men and women adopt different attitudes before "limit situations: they'll perceive it either as an obstacle they cannot overcome, or as one they do not (yet) wish to overcome, or still, as something they know exists and needs to be gotten through, thus, making them dedicate themselves to overcoming it."[4]

Untested feasibility is a practical proposition in overcoming, at least partially, the oppressive aspects perceived within reality. The risk of embracing the struggle for untested feasibility is a result of critical consciousness and its utopian nature, which makes the act of collectively dreaming a transformative movement. That is so because "when conscious beings want it, reflect, and act toward bringing down *limit situations* ... *untested feasibility* is no longer itself, but rather becomes its own concretization in what it had of unfeasible before."[5] Critical consciousness is not only predisposed to embracing change, but also engaged in the struggle for building untested feasibility—that is, "something known to exist by the utopian dream but that will only be attained through liberating praxis … something untested, not yet fully known and lived, but dreamed of."[6]

To dream is to imagine horizons of possibilities; to dream collectively is to embrace the struggle toward the building of conditions for possibility. The capacity for dreaming collectively, when embraced as a choice for radically living a common dream, constitutes an educational attitude oriented not only by the belief that *limit situations* can be altered, but, fundamentally, by the belief that this change is built constantly and collectively through the critical exercise of unveiling social *issues-problems* in question. The act of dreaming collectively, within the dialectics of denunciation and annunciation and within the commitment to building that overcoming, brings in itself an important educational/transformational potential. That potential both produces and is produced by untested feasibility, given that the impossible becomes transitory to the extent that we take collective responsibility for authoring *possible dreams.*

It should be emphasized, as a point of *obviousness,* that untested feasibility does not occur randomly, nor is it built individually, as well as the fact that creation of untested feasibility represents an alternative located in the realm of possibilities, not that of certainty. That is so since "the possibility/impossibility criterion for our dreams is a social-historical criterion, not an individual one."[7] Such is Freire's understanding, shown in his comprehension of *history as possibility* and of untested feasibility as a collectively built alternative based on critically living what is dreamed of. Collective dreaming, in a perspective of building untested feasibility, is, thus, a principle expressing practical possibilities for the intentional *Daring to Dream*.

Viewed this way, *Daring to Dream* is also a *Pedagogy of Conscientization* (the building of awareness and conscience) considering that Freire asserted his understanding as to its present-day relevance, "against all the force of the fatalist neoliberal discourse ... as an effort in the critical discovery of obstacles."[8] It is a pedagogy containing within itself the possibility for overcoming traditionally instituted and largely unquestioned practices, as it orients the development of a critical educational attitude where the distance between what is dreamed of and what is realized is conceived of as a space to be filled by the creative act. Taking collective responsibility for this creational space opens up room for solidifying transformative and untested feasible propositions.

Not of lesser importance is Freire's "admonition" to educators committed to liberating education: "misfortunate will be the ones among us who lose their capacity for dreaming, for inventing their own courage to denounce and announce."[9] Collective dreaming is thus a challenge put to all men and women who fight for *reinventing* education, in a democratic perspective, both in schools and in other educational spaces. It is by considering all these instances of *obviousness* constituted not only in the study of Paulo Freire's work but also in the effective—and affective—commitment to social practices that recreate it, that I have the pleasure to underscore the relevance of the discussion proposed by Nita—Ana Maria Araújo Freire—as she organizes this volume. It is a relevant discussion because it challenges us toward developing new theoretical and practical syntheses around Paulo Freire's work while reiterating one of its fundamental principles, that *changing is difficult, but possible and urgent.* I would especially like to thank Nita for her loving invitation to preface this book, provoking me toward the currency of this reflection, as well as allowing me to expand on interlocutions that mobilize untested feasible practices.

The reading of the works presented in this volume, developing the *Daring to Dream* theme, is a great contribution toward current popular education's potential as a reference of an educational practice integrated with a broader social movement, as it embraces the political task of *making the impossible possible.* That task constitutes a challenge to the Left in this country and in the world, as proposed by Marta Harnecker: "To the left, politics must consist, thus, in the art of discovering potentialities available in the concrete situation of today in order to make possible tomorrow what seems impossible at present."[10] However, this *pedagogical militancy* cannot lack in the struggle for the right to exercise the *beauty* of the educative act, much valued by Freire, as he argued for the need to recover hope, the joy of learning, curiosity, creative imagination, and the joy of teaching.

These and other types of knowledge demarcate the *wholeness* of the educator in living out his or her option for *Daring to Dream*. That is what we gain from reading this work Nita presents for the exercise of our *epistemological curiosity*.

My wishes are for a good reading that I hope can instigate us, in different ways, to give continuity to the collective movement for reflection-action and to systematic records as to *possible dreams* being constituted as daily challenges to the practice are faced up to. I do not wish this to be some nostalgic act of homage paid to Paulo Freire, but rather see it as an expression of political, epistemological, and aesthetic commitment to living liberating education. Finally, I hope we can go on learning, along with Nita, to transform the pain of our losses into a fertile movement of struggle for building social conditions favorable to the feasibility of *possible dreams*.

Ana Lúcia Souza de Freitas,
professora da Faculdade de Educação
da Pontifícia Universidade Católica
do Rio Grande do Sul

ENDNOTES

1. Paulo Freire, "Educação: O sonho possível," In *O educador: vida e morte*, 3d ed., ed. Carlos Rodrigues Brandão (Rio de Janeiro: Edições Graal, 1983), 92.

2. III National Conference of Education Supervisors, held in Goiânia, between October 20 and 25, 1980.

3. Freire, "Educação," 100.

4. Ana Maria Araújo Freire, "Notes," in Paulo Freire, *Pedagogia da esperança: um reencontro com a Pedagogia do oprimido* (Rio de Janeiro: Paz e Terra, 1992), 205.

5. Freire, "Notes," 207.

6. Freire, "Notes," 206.

7. Freire, "Educação," 99.

8. Paulo Freire, *Pedagogia da autonomia: saberes necessários à prática educativa* (São Paulo: Paz e Terra, 1996), 60.

9. Freire, "Educação," 101.

10. Marta Harnecker, *Tornar possivel o impossivel: a esquerda no limiar do século XXI* (São Paulo: Paz e Terra, 2000), 337.

FOREWORD

Peter Park

⟳

A well-known quote from Einstein has it that imagination is more important than knowledge. Einstein was interested not only in the physical world, the understanding of which he revolutionized, but also in the social, as is evident from his life-long adherence to socialism. His imagination was about dreaming of possible worlds and a new way of understanding them. In putting imagination before knowledge Einstein was dreaming of alternatives guided by the search for beauty. To him beauty in thought and in dreaming of new orders of things was more important than practicality that is tied to the present. In this sense he was a utopian.

In the United States, where dreaming is being snuffed out of children in the name of No Child Left Behind (NCLB), it is especially critical that we dare to dream.

This federally mandated educational program ended up forcing schools to teach to test on a narrow curriculum, most often centered around reading and math, and, in some cases, neglecting even the sciences. Under this pressure, schools are dropping arts, humanities, and sociocultural studies, which are the crucible of dreaming beautiful dreams. At the same time, incidentally, it has increased, rather than decreased, the inequality between the well-to-do and the poor, thus betraying the original vision behind the program. Critical thinking, which was promoted in the eighties and nineties, is talked about less and less under these circumstances, not only in elementary, middle, and high schools but also in higher education. Critical thinking, as opposed to critical theory or critical pedagogy, often ends up being training in the calculus of thinking and reasoning, rather than opening up vistas for a better world. Nevertheless, it at least offered opportunities for examining what is given with quizzical eyes. Even this limited avenue to contemplating new possibilities, however, is now being blocked, as education is becoming more and more testing, training, and taming.

To say that imagination is more important than knowledge is, of course, not to deny that we should pursue knowledge, for after all human life would be impossible without knowing. On this topic, Paulo was always emphatic that teachers must know the subject matters that they teach, and that teaching is not about pedagogical methods only, Freirean or otherwise, but must have contents. But there are different ways of understanding knowing. In the West, knowing has come to be defined narrowly as comprehending and representing the world and the objects in it as an outsider observing detached entities. This approach applies not only to physical objects but also to living things, including human beings. This way of thinking of knowledge, which began in Europe roughly five centuries ago, is very much tied to practicality and instrumentality in everyday life and is useful in this sense. It is the basis of modern science and technology, and it grew up together with capitalism, which in turn has valued it and supported it for its utility. There is thus a tight symbiosis between this representational mode way of knowing and modern capitalism The curriculum being encouraged under NCLB and other educational curricula tied to the so-called back-to-basics movement, the spirit of which NCLB embodies, are intended to go with this representational epistemological bent and fits like hand-in-glove with the current capitalist political economic arrangements prevailing not only in the United States but across the globe. It creates, when pursued alone, nondreaming, docile work forces for the postindustrial order.

But this way of knowing, which I have called representational elsewhere, is not the only form of knowledge that we acquire, posses, and practice. Surely knowing what is right and wrong in the moral sense is also something that we recognize in everyday life as knowing, however strange it may sound to today's objectivity-imbued ears. Grown-ups with responsibility and autonomy have the ability to judge right from wrong and act accordingly. But to the modern consciousness saturated in current scientific ethos, such ability has nothing to do with knowing, but more with innate disposition, habits, indoctrination, or even superstition and downright ir-rationality. This comes from the modern-day habit of mind which opposes fact to value, mind to body, head to heart, and knowing to feeling, in disregard of the mounting evidence that such dichotomies are not tenable philosophically. Knowing in general is entangled in desire and other kinds of feelings and being able to judge right from wrong is no exception. But this kind of knowing is banished from schools, starting with the injunction not to make value judgments. This is not to argue that snap judgments are always right. Quite the contrary. Judgments must be based on careful and sustained reflection and practice carried out in social settings, resulting in what might be termed reflective knowledge. Freirean dialogue embodies this way of knowing and Paulo's utopia is very much tied to it. It comes out of the desire for a possible better world based on realistic assessment of prevailing unsatisfactory social conditions and sustained cultural practice, which includes social action.

To Paulo, dreaming of a better world is not fantasy but is founded in clear understanding of the reality we live in and in contemplating what is possible. He used to say that we must walk with one foot in the here-and-now and another in utopia, physically imitating a person walking awkwardly straddling a small fence or a gutter. If he opposes dreaming to fatalism, which consigns the exploited, the weak, and dispossessed to doom, he also insists on distinguishing hopefulness from optimism, since dreams sometimes don't come true and we must work hard to attain them, often putting up with frustrations. Dreaming is very much a part of autonomy which we must exercise as fully grown and responsible human beings, or learn to do so as we grow up from our childhood, or as we liberate ourselves from our oppression. Autonomy is not a gift but something we must strive for and learn to exercise with reflective knowledge.

This slim volume brings together many of Paulo's thoughts and ideas running through his entire productive years, almost to the very end of his life. We have already encountered these ideas in his abundant publications and the numerous talks he gave in different parts of the world. But as I read the assembled pieces here, I notice with pleasure how his mode of discourse frees itself over the years from the tethers of academia and becomes more personal, intimate, and relational. This is the Paulo that I remember most fondly. His humanity comes shining through in these pieces, capturing his oral presentations, including a dialogue with young students and talks given at conferences. He delights in using colloquial expressions when called for, admits being afraid of public speaking, readily shows his sorrow in losing his beloved first wife, and openly declares his romantically youthful love for his new one. In the dialogue with the students, he starts out feeling tired and weak, then gains strength as he interacts with the students, picking up energy from the encounter. This was his characteristic way of relating to the people he was addressing, whether in private or public, and this style comes through here strongly. The talks captured here make it abundantly clear that they are impromptu performances, composed on his feet, or literally from the seat of his pants, as must have often been the case, which he openly admits in some places. I used to think that his speaking had a faintly poetic twist to it when he spoke publicly in English, because this was not his native tongue, and he had to use his linguistic inventiveness. But some of this quality is also audible in the pieces he "spoke," as he used to call it, even when, as we see it here, they were originally delivered in Portuguese, his beloved language, and rendered into English. It is as if he is composing poems right in front of his audience regardless of what language he is speaking. This is another way by which he brings intimacy to people and becomes relational. This aspect of the power of his pedagogy is often not recognized. The Freirean pedagogy surely creates representational knowledge about the social world that we live in. But his was also a pedagogy of love which he practiced in his writing and oral deliveries as well as in relating to people. He often spoke of the importance of love in teaching—love between teacher and student and, ultimately, love among human beings. Love is the most sublime expression of relating with and knowing another person. This kind of knowledge derives from and resides in human relationships. Call this relational knowledge. This is another kind of knowing which we recognize as such in everyday language and practice, but that the modern mind excludes it from epistemology and banishes it from schools. Paulo may not have explicitly acknowledged that his pedagogy is founded in relational knowing, for the concept and the terminology would have been foreign to him as they are to many of us, but the idea is clearly manifested in the method he invented and practiced. And the immanence of relational knowing in Freirean pedagogy is made more apparent in the oral nature of many of the pieces we see in this volume, which allows his intimate style of interacting to come through, thus co-creating relational knowledge with his readers.

The editor of this volume, Ana Maria Araújo Freire (Nita), has done a felicitous job of selecting essays from Paulo's unpublished papers and assembling them here to show the side of Freirean pedagogy that does not easily come through in texts intended as written communication. We owe her congratulations and enormous gratitude.

Peter Park
Professor Emeritus,
University of Massachusetts at Amherst and
Adjunct Professor, University of Colorado at Boulder
May 31, 2007

POETRY BY PAULO FREIRE

From Ana Maria Araújo Freire's Collection

⟜

Some time after his arrival
the foreigner said to the men in the valley
one dusking afternoon:
Thus far I have spoken to you only
of the songs of birds and
of the tenderness of the dawns.
It was necessary to undertake with you some
fundamental learning:
to feel the uncertainty of tomorrow,
living out the negation of myself,
through a work that is not our own.
Only so, speaking to you would be a form of
speaking with you.
Now I can tell you:
We do not believe in those who proclaim
that our weakness is a gift from the Gods,

that it is in us as the fragrance in the flowers
or the dew in the mornings.
Our weakness is not the ornament
of our bitter lives.
We do not believe in those who state,
in hypocritical intonation,
that life is really like this
—a few having so much,
millions having nothing.
Our weakness is not a virtue.
Let us pretend, however, that we do believe
in their discourse.
It is important that not a gesture of ours
reveal our true intention.
It is important that they leave happy in their
lie,
certain that we are things of their own.
We need time
to prepare our own discourse
that will shake up mountains and valleys,
rivers and oceans
and that will leave them stunned and fearful.
Our different discourse
—our action-word—will be spoken
by our whole bodies:
our hands, our feet, our reflections.
All within us will speak
a life-bearing language
—even the instruments that
our hands will use,
when, in communion, we

shall transform our weakness
into our strength.
Poor us, however, if we cease to speak
simply because they can no longer lie.
Therefore, I tell you:
Our liberation discourse
Is not the medicine for a passing illness.
If we go silent as the present lies quiet down,
new lies will appear,
in the name of our liberation.
Our different discourse
—our action-word—
As a true discourse
will be made and remade;
it never is or will have been,
because it will always be being.
Our different discourse
—our action-word—
must be a permanent one.

Paulo Freire
Geneva
April 1971

PART I

COMMENTARIES AND ESSAYS

I

IMPOSSIBLE TO EXIST WITHOUT DREAMS[1]

⊷

I believe that, as progressive educators, we have the ethical responsibility to reveal situations of oppression. I believe it is our duty to create the means to under-standing political and historical realities so as to bring about the possibility of change. I feel it is our role to develop work methods that allow the oppressed to, little by little, reveal their own reality.

At this point in history, it seems that there are certain responsibilities that fall to us. Recently, reactionary forces have obtained success in proclaiming the disappearance of ideologies and the advent of a new history, one devoid of social classes and, therefore, without antagonistic interests or class struggle. At the same time, they maintain that there is no need to keep talking about dreams, utopia, or social justice. However, to me, *it is impossible to live without dreams.* How can we accept these neoliberal discourses which have been preached as if they were real and also keep our dreams alive? One way to accomplish that, I believe, is to awaken the political consciousness of educators.

Neoliberal doctrine seeks to limit education to technological practice. Currently, education is no longer understood as formative, but simply as training. I feel we must keep on creating alternative work models. If implemented in a critical manner, educational practice can make an invaluable contribution to the political struggle. Educational practice is not the only path toward the social transformation necessary for conquering human rights; however, without it, I believe, there will never be social transformation. Education manages to provide people with greater clarity in "reading the world," and that clarity opens up the possibility for political intervention. Such clarity is what will pose a challenge to neoliberal fatalism.

The language of neoliberals speaks about the need for unemployment, for poverty, for inequality. I feel it is a duty of ours to fight against such fatalistic mechanical forms of comprehending history. So long as people attribute the hunger and poverty that destroy them to destiny, to fatality, or to God, there will be little chance to promote collective action. Likewise, if we allow ourselves to fall for the trickery of neoliberal economic discourses, which affirm realities of homelessness and poverty as inevitable, then opportunities for change become invisible, and our role in fostering change becomes absent. In my view, "being" in the world means to transform and re-transform the world, not to adapt to it. As human beings, there is no doubt that our main responsibilities consist of intervening in reality and keeping up our hope. While progressive educators, we must be committed to those responsibilities. We have to apply ourselves to creating a context in which people can question the fatalistic perceptions of the circumstances where they find themselves, so that we can all fulfill our role as participants in history.

TOWARD A "PEDAGOGY OF DESIRE"

Let us take, for example, the work done with people who live on the streets. I surround myself with caution when speaking about specific cases, since every context is different, and I do not believe in prescriptive approaches. In order to develop work alternatives in every situation, we have to go to the people involved and discuss together what needs to be done in their context. Nevertheless, in all contexts, through language and actions, I am interested in finding ways to create a context where people who live on the streets can reconstruct their wishes and desires—a desire to start again or just to start being in different ways. I am interested in the creation of a *pedagogy of desire.*

As progressive educators, one of our main tasks seems to be with respect to generating political dreams in people, political yearnings, political desires. It is impossible for me, as an educator, to build up the yearnings of other men and women. That task is theirs, not mine. In what way can we find work alternatives that provide a favorable context for that to happen?

As I seek to develop a pedagogy of desire, I am in-terested in exploring possibilities for making it clear that living on the streets is not a "natural" event but rather a social, historical, political, and economic event. I am interested in exploring the reasons for living on the streets. This type of investigation will lead us to some discoveries. We might discover that people do not live on the streets because they want to. Still, they might come to realize that indeed they want to stay on the streets, but then, they might engage in a different kind of questioning, seeking to find out why they want things that way, seeking the origins of such desire.

In that type of search, the search for reasons, we prepare ourselves and others to overcome a fatalistic understanding of our own situations, of our contexts. Overcoming a fatalistic understanding of history neces-sarily means discovering the role of consciousness, of subjectivity in history. Overcoming fatalistic compre-hensions as to "being" on the street is synonymous to probing the social, political, and historic reasons for being on the streets—against which we can fight, in this way, collectively and consciously.

BEYOND CHARITY

It is necessary to establish an important distinction be-tween that process and charity. In the campaign against hunger launched by sociologist Herbert de Souza, Betinho, assistance has been provided to some needy people in the form of food. However, in Brazil alone, there are thirty-three million people who starve. There is absolutely no possibility that charitable initiatives alone can solve the problem of hunger. In order to solve this problem, we need to understand the relationships between hunger and food production, food production and land reform, land reform and reaction against it, hunger and economic policy, hunger and violence, and hunger while violence, hunger and democracy. We will have to realize that victory over destitution and hunger is a political struggle in support of profound transformation in the structures of society.

For that reason, we need to approach problems in such a manner as to invite people to understand the relationship between the problem and other factors, like politics and oppression. I believe that is what the campaign against hunger is doing. It is making hunger into a shocking, embarrassing, and revolting presence among us. I have no doubt that Betinho never did intend to simply organize a charitable campaign. The campaign has provided assistance in a manner that feeds the curiosity of the "assisted." That seems crucial. Gradually, it has made it viable to them to accept themselves as subjects of history, through their involvement in the political struggle. It is up to us to make history and to be made and remade by it. Only by making history in a different manner, will we be able to put an end to hunger.

RECOGNIZING GRASSROOTS WORK AND IMAGINING THE FUTURE

As subjects capable of promoting change, at times we do not notice changes that are in progress. Sometimes we do not realize the grassroots work we do with our sights on awakening revolutionary consciousness. Sometimes we fail to recognize the importance of that work and the potential for change that can be developed from it. For example, let us look at the advances made by the popular movements throughout the 1980s and at the beginning of the 1990s, a decade many considered lost. Look at all the advances that the landless have accomplished in this country [Brazil]. They experienced many victories in their struggle for land rights, while working the land under the regime of cooperatives and creating camps. This movement, which now counts on tremendous popular support, has a long history. Its popularity has increased a great deal in the past ten years, but its origins reach back to a distant past in Brazilian history. One of its many origins is in the kilombos[2] created hundreds of years ago by Brazilian blacks of African origin who resisted against slavery. The kilombos were places where the black slaves of Brazil found refuge, living in community, on the basis of solidarity. The slaves who organized this resistance created practically self-supporting cities and, in doing so, created an alternative and symbolic country. They fought against the white state hundreds of years ago. They manifested the Brazilian desire for life and for freedom, presently synthesized, in fantastic ways, by the Movement of Landless Rural Workers (MST).

It is hard to imagine what directions MST will take. The landless count on very strong political consciousness. They know their project. They are beginning to invite the unemployed to join them in the struggle. They know what must be done—today or in the future.

I am sure that they also know what will be necessary in order to involve those who live on the streets. They know that land reform will, if not immediately, at least in ten years, count on the support of the people who live in the streets of cities.

About three or four years ago, I had the opportunity to teach a closing class to a group of young popular educators on a farm that had been successfully claimed by MST. The following day, the educators would part ways and go on to the different camps the farm had been divided into. At a given moment, a young man who worked with literacy and was a very active voice in the movement spoke to all of us. In his speech he said, "During one of the initial moments of our struggle, we had to cut, with the strength we gained in our union, the barbed wire that surrounded this farm. We cut it and went in. However, after we entered, we came to realize that, in the process of rupture of physical barriers, we had also cut other chains, other fences. We were cutting through the shackles of illiteracy, of ignorance, and of fatalism. Our ignorance makes for the happiness of landowners, the same way that our learning, our reading, the improvement to our memory, and the advances we have accomplished culturally make those same landowners tremble in fear. We now know that it is not enough to turn the land into economic production centers for all of us, we must also turn it into centers of culture, of learning."

Today, it seems possible that the landless are capable of promoting real changes and of transforming this country without violence. It seems to me like a time of great possibilities. The progressive educators of the past played their role in bringing us to this point, in revealing practices of oppression and injustice. We still have crucial roles to play. We must envision our work with a base on a sense of perspective and history. Our struggle of today does not mean that we will necessarily accomplish changes, but without this fight, today, the future generations may have to struggle a great deal more. History does not end with us; it continues on.

ENDNOTES

1. *Kilombos,* spelled *quilombos* in Portuguese, are communities created by escaped slaves that survived for generations in hiding in Brazil.

2. This piece was originally published in Australia, under the title "Contribuir para a historia e reveler a oppressão," in *Dulwich Center Journal* 3 (1999): 37–39. The translation is by Klauss Brandini Gerhardt. The commentary was recorded at Paulo Freire's house in São Paulo on April 24, 1997. David Denborough and Cheryl White, who work for an organization providing aid to the homeless, were present, in addition to Walter Varanda.

2

ON THE COGNITIONAL ACT[1]

⤙

At this moment, as educators from different Latin American countries, we find ourselves gathered in a common search.

The intent of the organization sponsoring this conference, and it must coincide with that of those assembled here, is to carry out a cognitional act.

Thus, it becomes an imposition that all those sharing this attitude, or inclined toward sharing it, demarcate the cognizable object upon which we will be exercising the cognitional act.

This first requirement implies the indeclinable necessity that the act, for which we are more than just preparing ourselves, since we already feel inserted in it, not be reduced to a mere "running" of the eyes, without commitment, with little or naïve curiosity, over what will be the object of our reflectional incidence. An uncritical "running" of the eyes, as if the object of our analysis were something we should just blabber about and, thus, would not be capable of provoking within us a penetrating and restless degree of curiosity.

Since we are dealing with a cognitional act, we have to, from the very moment we seek to identify its object, carry out an "ad-miration" of something that, while being "ad-mirable" at a given moment, will become an *ad-mired* object, thus, cognizable incidence of our cognizability.

The implication here is that the true cognitional act places the subject in a perceptive position before "ad-mirables" that is different in nature from that of those not capable of the qualitative transformation of "ad-mirable" into "ad-mired."

The fundamental qualitative change here resides in the fact that, in the first case, the object remaining on the "ad-mirable" level becomes present to the subject's perception, but as something he or she takes notice of, while in the second case, by identifying the object as an "ad-mired," the cognitional subject penetrates, or moves deeper and deeper into, the *ontos* of the object.

In the first hypothesis, the subject will merely have an opinion about the "ad-mirable"; in the second, he or she will have knowledge. Taking notice of the "ad-mirable" is *doxa*; penetrating the "ad-mired" and reaching its *ontos* is *logos*.

There is, however, more change of a qualitative character in the passage from "ad-mirable" to "ad-mired." That is, the object, now already "ad-mired" or in process of "ad-miration," becomes able to mediate the "ad-miration" of the subjects who focus their reflection on it. That way, by penetrating, taking notice of, "apprehending" it, as they attain its intelligibility, the cognitional subjects establish their communicability.

It is just that without a cognizable reality—ad-mired or in the process of ad-miration—that mediates cognitional subjects around which dialogically shared knowledge is established, as [Edouard] Nicol would say, there would be no intelligibility or, as a consequence, communicability.

In the cognitional exercise we have been attempting, it seems that the first serious operation put to us is the critical perception of the linguistic structure that was offered for our analysis: "The role of education as one of the priority means in the process of cultural change."

What do we do now to satisfy the need to place ourselves before the ad-mired object in order to know it? Or, still, what might the object be upon which we will focus our ad-miration, our cognitional act?

Undoubtedly, we are before a linguistic structure where the signifiers necessarily signify as a function of the position they occupy in the contextual structure.

However, because they are signified signifiers, that is, because they are, while meanings, interrelated signals, they are language-thought referring to the world.

It will thus be by starting from the perception of the message included in the language-thought, undeniably represented in the proposed linguistic structure, that we will delineate the object that must be the focus of our cognizability, at this moment.

Either from a naive or from a critical point of view, we can state the unquestionable existence of a fundamental theme, or themes, objects of our cognizability, in the position presented.

The difference between one position and the other lies in how the cognitional subject approaches the linguistic structure in order to apprehend, in the language-thought referring to the world, the cognitional theme.

While the unguarded or naive consciousness would tend to expose one or another of the angles detectable in the linguistic context, without establishing the dialectic relationship between what is detectable in the linguistic context and reality, the critical consciousness will lean toward the apprehension of the ad-mired through "'abstraction and generalization of the linguistic signals.'"

The former, in the best of scenarios, would be satisfied with a purely grammatical analysis of the proposition; the latter starts from knowing that perception of the signals in the text will only be possible to the extent that the real context, the concrete objective situation where the phenomenon the words refer to takes place, is noticed.

Thus, the naive consciousness, while being abstract, does not engage in abstraction, whereas the critical one, while concretely inserted in reality, engages in abstraction in order to know.

That means, precisely, that the abstraction the critical mind engages in to attain knowledge implies no rupture from objective situations, but contrarily, a move closer to them.

Abstraction, in that sense, is the operation through which the subject, in a truly cognitional act, in a way removes a fact, a concrete element from the real context where it takes place, and subjects it to ad-miration in a theoretical context. The subject, then, exercises his or her cognizability onto the object, transforming it from "ad-mirable" to "ad-mired." In reality, what happens now, in the theoretical context, is a re-ad-miration of the previous ad-miration carried out by the subject when in direct relationship with the empirical.

If the ad-miration of the real carried out by the subject, one that implies a *distancing* from the object by him or her, aimed at making it objective, transforming it, and knowing it, so that he or she can be *with* it, the re-ad-miration of the ad-miration, which takes place in the theoretical context, implies not only recognition of the previous knowledge but also knowledge of why one knows.

Now, then, there is no doubt that all of us here in this space and moment find ourselves within a theoretical context in the exact sense of the word. Here, it is up to us, as it has been since the beginning of this conference, and even before, when it was being prepared, to engage in the serious effort of re-ad-miration. But what to re-ad-mire? After all, what will we have to place before ourselves, before our restless curiosity for knowing? What ad-mirable will here become an ad-mired, so that we can further penetrate it, further move into it, while the more we do it, the more we know we will always have to restart?

"The role of education as one of the priority means in the process of cultural change"; here is the text whose significance, never dichotomized from the reality in which we are, shall bring to us the object of our reflection.

Even though the text presents itself, in its total significance, as quite a bit categorically affirmative, it seems doubtless to us that the fundamental issue being revealed to us as ad-mired is a discussion between education and cultural change.

What we must re-admire now is education as indeed a *to-do* of men and women, precisely for that reason, a *what-to-do* that takes place within the domain of culture and of history.

Since every re-ad-miration act implies the perception of a previous perception of the same act, which results or not in a change of behavior as part of the perception associated with it, let us attempt, as is valid in the theoretical situation we are in, to revisit the educational *what-to-do* as it takes or has been taking place among us.

From this re-view, this re-ad-miration, we will observe:

a. whether education has been indeed one of the priority means in the process of cultural change, or whether, to the contrary, it has been an efficient instrument for status quo maintenance;

b. whether education can really come to be a transformation factor toward the liberation of men and women;

c. and how it will erect itself into this force for cultural transformation given that it is, at the same time, an expression of culture.

If there is one thing we are not afraid to state, in this re-ad-miration effort, is that even the simplest look at education, provided it is not simplistic, naive, or preconceived, as a systematic *what-to-do* among us, at any level, reveals in great detail the not always deliberate (which does not matter in our analysis) character of the sense of education as an instrument of domination.

The educator–learner relationships whose contradiction is not overcome result in educators always being the ones who educate and the learners the ones who are educated; the former are the ones who think and the latter the ones "thought" (become the object of the educators' thinking)—those the educators who discipline and these the learners who are disciplined. The educators are the ones who select the instructional content and the learners, as passive beings, are the ones who are filled with that content. The educators are, then, the subjects; the learners are the objects in the process.

In fact, the educators who speak about the adaptive purpose of education are not few, as if men and women, as beings of praxis, therefore, also beings of transformation, of re-creation, and of reinvention, were to be tied to a reality which, in turn, is as unfinished as men and women remain unfinished and which only is because it is being.

To speak of adapting men and women to a reality that, in being human, can only be historical-cultural, since for men and women there is no *here* that isn't also *now*, is to negate the very continuity of history and culture.

What is there, really, in this educative *to-do,* in elementary or secondary schools, in universities, mostly with lecture classes, which seem more like sleepy lullabies, that might enable learners to perceive themselves perceiving?

What liberating dimension might exist in practices that inhibit creativity and lead the learner to "bureaucratized" repetitions of the not-always brilliant discourses of their "masters"?

How to have creativity if the learner is forbidden from running the risk of the creative adventure?

How can we reconcile the authentically cognitional act with the so-called reading controls, which are actually controls of people? Those controls are exercised, in painful irony, in the name of the learners' need to study!

How can a cultural exchange be encouraged when, from the start, the young are considered petulant for putting all shades of bureaucracy to the canvas of judgment?

How can this education establish itself as an instrument for cultural change if it finds it fundamental to imprison time?

What role might this education play toward change if, as a product of a culture of domination, it encourages and enables the introjection of domination, rather than problematizing the very culture of which it is a product?

What liberating significance can an educational *to-do* have when it sees in the popular masses minor beings and when it starts from the a priori that they must be guided, as absolutely incapable? Further, since there is nothing that does not have its opposite, if the popular masses need to be guided; it is because there are those who guide them.

Where is the effort toward cultural change in those patronizing literacy campaigns that lost themselves in the mechanical repetitions of ba-be-bi-bo-bu[2] and in the readings of "Eva saw the grape," of "the bird has a wing"? Where is the effort toward cultural change in those readers who ask whether "Ada gave her finger to the vulture" or those who tell poor men and women that "it is better to have a plate of a few beans given out of love than a steak gained through fighting"?

Where is the commitment to changing in an education that sees the search for the Being More as subversive and views dehumanization as the order that must be established?

[...]

ENDNOTES

1. The ideas in this unfinished piece were, as the reader can verify, later reworked in *Pedagogia do oprimido,* a work started that same year of 1967, in Chile, and in "Ação cultural para a liberdade e outros escritos," in 1969, in the *Harvard Educational Review.*

2. *Ba-be-bi-bo-bu* refers to the traditional way that Brazilians learn how to read and write, and the sentences between quotes are examples taken from a traditional manual.

3

HISTORY AS POSSIBILITY[1]

⮂

At the end of a century that is also the end of a millennium, touched and challenged by world wars, by local wars of an almost global character, by radical transformations of a social, political, economic, ideological, ethical nature, by revolutions in science and technology, by the overcoming of beliefs, of myths, by the return to doubt that puts in judgment an exceedingly certain certainty in modernity, it is not easy to catalogue all that may seem to us fundamentally problematic and that men and women of the nascent century will soon have to respond to. The challenges of this end of century carry into the next one.

Some points of unquestionable complexity, which involve from politics to epistemology, can be inventoried.

1. North–South relations. While a center of power, the North has gotten used to profiling the South. The North "*norteia*."[2] One of the tasks that the South will impose on itself in those relations is that of, while overcoming its dependence, starting to "*sulear*,"[3] and, thus, to stop always being "*norteado*." The unbalance between North and South ends up affecting the North's own interests and hurting the advance of democracy.

2. The problem of hunger in the world—more than a horrid reality, a resounding obscenity.

3. The problem of violence, not only physical and direct violence, but also that of a more shifty and symbolic nature: violence and hunger, violence and economic interests, violence and racism, violence and sexism.

4. The rebirth, not only in Europe, but the world over, more emphatically here, less so there, of the fascist threat, as if the world had lost its memory.

5. The astonishment of the *Lefts* before the fall of the so-called realist socialism—to me much more an act of rebellion, an ode to liberty, than the death of socialism—and their tendency to:

    a. buy into the neoliberal discourse that speaks of the death of *ideologies,* of *history,* and of *social classes,* that speaks of the death of utopias, of dreams, and of socialism as being unviable;

    b. not recognize that the evils of the socialist experiment lay with the authoritarian, Stalinist framework with which it was imposed, while the positives of capitalism lies in the democratic framework in which it moves, thus reactivating Stalinism, unbearable negativity.

In reality, the role of the Lefts today is not to believe that they already exist or must remain authoritarian, "religious," but rather to overcome their historical, philosophical, political, epistemological errors, such as, for example, that of antagonizing socialism and democracy.

6. This end of century brings back the importance of the role of subjectivity as a philosophical, historical, epistemological, political, pedagogical problem, which has as much to do with modern physics as with educational practice, with knowledge theory as with democracy. After all, the topic of subjectivity was always present in human concerns and is now revived, overcoming a certain mechanicism of Marxist origin—but not solely of Marx's responsibility—which reduced subjectivity to a mere reflex of objectivity, preventing, in the same way, the repetition of naiveties that made that importance absolute and that resulted in lending to subjectivity or to consciousness the role of maker of the world. One of the ghastly consequences of that mechanistic understanding of subjectivity was an equally mechanistic intelligence of history, one deterministic in nature, where the future was viewed as inexorable, *virgin,* therefore, stripped of any *problematics.* It is in history as *possibility* that subjectivity, in a dialectic-contradictory relationship with objectivity, takes on the role of subject rather than simply object of world transformations.

The future, then, stops being inexorable and becomes what it is historically: *problematic.*

São Paulo, August 16, 1993

ENDNOTES

1. This piece was written by Paulo Freire at the request of Radiotelevisão Portuguesa, on August 16, 1993.

2. Translator's note: In Portuguese there is the verb *nortear* that comes from the word for *north, norte,* and means "to guide or provide direction." For more on the ideology of "nortear," see Márcio Campos in "Notes" by Ana Maria Araújo Freire, in *Pedagogia da esperança: um reencontro com a Pedagogia do oprimido* (Rio de Janeiro: Paz e Terra, 1992), 218–21, n. 15.

3. Translator's note: *Sulear* is a Freire neologism based on the Portuguese word *sul* for *south,* meant to oppose the word *nortear* as explained in the previous note.

4

A FEW REFLECTIONS AROUND
UTOPIA[1]

✺

I never speak about utopia as an impossibility that might, at times, work out. Even more so, I do not ever speak about utopia as the refuge of those who do not take action or [as] the unreachable pronunciation of those who can only fantasize. I speak of utopia, on the contrary, as a fundamental necessity for human beings. It is part of their historically and socially constituted nature that men and women, under normal conditions, must not do without dreaming and utopia. Fatalist ideologies are, for that very reason, negating of the peoples, of women, and of men.

As beings programmed for learning[2] and who need *tomorrow* as fish need water, men and women become robbed" beings if they are denied their condition of participants in the production of tomorrow. Every tomorrow, however, that is thought about, and for whose realization there is a struggle, necessarily implies dreaming and utopia. There is no tomorrow without a project, without a dream, without utopia, without hope, without creative work, and work toward the development of possibilities, which can make the concretization of that tomorrow viable. It is in that sense that I have said on different occasions that I am hopeful not out of stubbornness, but due to an existential imperative. Therein is rooted the impetus, as well, with which I fight against all fatalism. I do not "turn a deaf ear" to the fatalist discourse of educators who, in light of the current obstacles associated with the globalization of the economy, reduce education solely to technique and proclaim the death of dreams, of utopia. If there are no social classes any longer, and consequently their conflicts, if there are no ideologies any longer, the Right and the Left, if development has no longer anything to do with politics, but only with a mean and greedy ethic, that of the market, if economic globalization has shortened the world, if the world has become more or less equal, what is left to education is pure *training* and *taming* of learners. I refuse this reactionary pragmatism, as much as the satisfied discourse of those who speak about starving Brazilians or about the unemployed of the world as "a fatality" of this end of century.

My discourse in favor of dreaming, of utopia, of freedom, of democracy is the discourse of those who refuse to settle and do not allow the taste for being human, which fatalism deteriorates, to die within themselves.

ENDNOTES

1. Previously unpublished Paulo Freire text, not dated.

2. François Jacob, "Nous sommes programmés mais pour apprendre," *Le Courrier* (UNESCO), February 1991.

PART II

DIALOGUES AND CONFERENCES

5

A CONVERSATION WITH STUDENTS[1]

⟶

PF: Well, it makes me happy to be here with you. My experience in teaching, lived a long time ago, had as one result the small book you have just read and involved teaching kids your age. But that was a long time ago. I am happy that you all have read some of my writings, and I will be spending some time here with you, now, to hear what you might have to say or ask. If I can, I will answer. So ... while you are not asking questions yet, I'll ask one, "Do you all like, or rather, are you enjoying reading? Reading this kind of reading instead of just a cartoon magazine or something like that? I think those should be read, too; I am not against them. But I would like to know if you also like to read a bigger book. Who has any experience with that?

Note: "PF" indicates the speaker is Paolo Freire.

St: Everybody.

PF: Everybody, because the schools themselves ask for that, is that right?

St: But as an obligation, and that is not cool....

PF: As an obligation ....

St: We have to have a book for school because they are requiring it; that is different from having a book that you wanted and chose because you like it.... It is much more interesting to read a book you have chosen yourself than one assigned at school.

PF: What if school changed a bit, and instead of requiring ....

St: I don't think what the school assigns is very interesting.

But every year there is one book that you get to choose....

PF: So the student gets to choose one reading?

St: There must be some objective for the books being assigned at school....

Yeah, you don't end up knowing only one kind of language; you have a chance to get to know other types through the books assigned at school.

For example, the seventh grade class is now reading a very Brazilian book. We often read books by

---

Note: "St" indicates the speaker is a student. New lines following after a speaker denoted "St" without the "St" appellation are different student speakers.

British authors, American authors, etc. I think most people are enjoying reading this book.

I think that the most interesting system for reading at school is the circulating library, because everybody can go there, choose the book they found interesting, say they are going to read it, and not as an obligation because they are choosing the books themselves, right? That way, it is always more possible that they will really like the books. It does everybody's head good....

PF: What does that mean, "to do everybody's head good"?

St: (laughter) ... Enjoying the book. Reading it from beginning to end, reading it for real.

A book that does not do it for your head, you skip more pages than you read, right?

PF: I would like to explain to you why I asked that. I have a number of reasons why I would ask what that means. But one of those reasons is this: I lived away from Brazil for sixteen years; I don't know if you all knew that. And because of this business of reading, writing, and also teaching people how to read and write, I was removed from the university and had to leave Brazil. I was gone away from here for sixteen years and could not even dream of coming back. But language does not stop; that's it; language does not stop; there is a constant process of change. Language goes on becoming richer. And this thing they call a tongue is indeed language;

it speaks. When I got back from exile in 1980, I found an expression that did not exist before: "to make one's head." I was quite terrified with that expression, horrified by what it means. That is why, just now, when you said "to make everybody's head," I asked what it meant. You guys gave an explanation that did not satisfy me. To me it is not exactly like wanting to read that book. What is it, "to make someone's head," *really?* Did the teacher "make the head" of the student ....

St: She exposed her opinion....

PF: Ahhh!

St: She convinced.... No, she did not convince, but it is like in your book when you say that teaching reading and writing is a political act. You do end up getting across what you think to those you are teaching.

PF: To get across what we think.... You said something important. I would like to ask another question. I will keep on asking these little questions, and then I'll tie it all together. You said I mentioned in the book that it is about getting across to the other what we believe, for example. Could it be that the role of the educator is that one, of making an effort to really get things across, or not? But getting across here not in the sense of taking it here and giving it over there, but rather of convincing.

St: I think the role of the teacher is to create a path.... Because I believe that the illiterate, and the adult ones in particular, while they cannot read or are not able to do any research or become informed so as to create their own opinions, end up going for the opinions of others. They end up accepting the impositions of others. Then, in the end, emptiness is created. So, the teacher gives you data so that you can think and open up your own path, without imposing anything.

PF: I believe that as well, imposing never. Not ever! But I ask you (let us try to pick up on some subtlety): One of the tasks, one of the obligations, is exactly this one you guys told me about, to open up a path—that is, to propose. And to show, for example, that up here on this table there are two tape recorders, but that besides that, there is something that is kept hidden from all of you over there; no one can see that in here there are three cassettes, better yet, three cassette cases, one with a tape in it and two without. In other words, in the world there are always hidden things; in life, there are always hidden things, and one of the roles of the educator is to draw attention to those things. Sometimes it is not even necessary to show the hidden thing, but rather it is about helping the student to know that there are hidden things for him or her to discover. That is what you called "opening up a path." But I don't know if you agree with me; I think there is also another task. I believe that, at the same time that I propose, that I open up paths, I fight to convince the student that I am right. Let me give you guys an example

I have found. In some programs in Europe or in the United States, some teachers, albeit fewer and fewer, that I can recall now, while teaching their classes, suggested that blacks are inferior to whites. One of those teachers said, "I am greatly saddened to have to say this. I only say it because it is science that is demonstrating that blacks are inferior to whites. There are, however, a few things here and there at which blacks are better, such as carrying weight at work or running." That is why, they believe in general, American blacks win in the Olympic Games. If I am a teacher as well and work with this teacher's students, I feel it is my duty to fight so that the students will not believe in that other teacher's science. That is, I feel obligated, and that I have a duty, to say this is a lie. And if it is a lie it is because I have another truth. Then, that is the other role of the educator, which is that of convincing, rather than stopping at his or her opinion, and of showing that his/her opinion is more than opinion, that it is a truth that can be accepted. I don't mean to believe, exactly, because there is no truth. I would see as the educator's important roles and tasks, then, those of opening up paths and of challenging, doing whatever it takes so that the students cannot fall asleep at the switch. Falling asleep here is not just meant from a physical point of view, in reality, but rather from the standpoint of becoming uninterested. On the one hand; to provoke, etc. And at the same time; to never omit. An educator can never hide before his or her students. He or she can never be ashamed of being an educator. In other words, he or she must assert him- or herself as an educator, as one who educates. It is the same thing with mothers. Can you imagine your mothers crossing their arms and saying, "I have nothing to do with that," or your fathers saying, "Don't pay too much attention to this stuff"? Of course, at your age it is actually a bit of a drag when your fathers and mothers start asking questions about who you are going out with today and what time you will be back.... But tomorrow you will know that those questions are necessary. Those questions only start to become unappealing when they become instruments for imprisoning teenagers. However, all in all, to finish up this part of our chat, I believe that the teacher's role is more than simply opening up a way. It is necessary, at times, that the educators have the courage to take responsibility for the job of showing the way. Now, I do agree with you all; to me, the duty of a democratic educator can never be that of someone who intends to domesticate the students and impose his/her own beliefs or political positions on them. For example, the soccer team I root for in São Paulo is Corinthians, but I cannot threaten my students: "Either you root for Corinthians, or I'll give you a zero!" It cannot be like that. Or something like: "Either you believe in God, or you'll all have 4!" That cannot be done. In other words, the educator has to respect the being, the way a boy or a girl is being. ? And how about the book? With respect to the reading you did, what questions would you put to me?

St: I found that part where you argue that reading is not just assimilating words interesting. Ever since someone is a child, you present reading as life. There can be a reading that is linked to living. You present an experience of your own, and all that clarified things for me, and there was a certain complicity with respect to what I felt as well.

We know what reading is, but we cannot say what it really is. We are even afraid of saying it: "No, I don't think reading is just that; it is much more." We are afraid that someone might say, "No, but I do not believe so." Then, when someone else puts that in a very clear way, and you realize that is it, you see the whole thing another way. You see that you were right, and you gain much more than before, since you know clearly what it is.

I would like to talk about the relationship you create between being and reading so that one can write. That is linked to your experience, to your living. You have to write, and at the same time, you have to be reading everything. You are reading and writing at the same time, right?

I thought that you explained well that reading is something natural. When I was reading, I felt that everything is to read, so you are born reading already. I had this thing in my head that you had to have a certain experience in order to be able to understand, that it was no use for them to keep teaching us things outside our own experience. I think that most people already had that idea. So, it was very interesting to see the confirmation of what we were already thinking in your work.

What made it much easier for me to understand is that I have to group, read along with other deciphering I do, with what I see, hear, smell, touch, right? It's about putting it all together. Reading is not just running your eyes over it. I have to live what it is that I am reading to be able to understand.

You know what else I found out as well? I later noticed that, while you are reading, your sensations increase. If you are able to comprehend what you are reading, when the guy says, "A green field, with a person over there," you don't just see a green field, but you feel that it can be in there as well.

And you can have a bunch of things because you are living things. It feels like you are at the place where the story is taking place. It seems like you are inside it, in the same period, living with the same characters, but you are just seeing it.... You put it together the way you can assimilate best. Every one has a different way to see the characters, for example, at a given place. And, even though the author can describe that place entirely, it becomes something completely different to other people....

That's why I find illustration cool.... Not the illustration in itself, but like Monteiro Lobato used to do, drawing something not completely. It may be something a bit vague, some shapes, right? For me to imagine a person in a book is a very personal thing; I do not imagine it just like the drawing. To me it is always a shape....

Film and illustration impose the author's mind somewhat....

That is why a book is much more interesting and cool than a movie.

A movie is like this: the guy who made that movie is the one who thinks it comes from the book. You have not read and don't know. I think it is cool to watch a movie of a book you have read to find out other people's opinion, to ask them what they think. But if you see the movie first and then read the book, it is no fun....

—It is not like you imagined....

Right, without illustration, a book cannot just hook the reader through the eyes. The illustration cuts down a bit on the reader's image, his or her creativity.

PF: Are you guys also having another activity proposed by your school, that is, do you enjoy writing as well?

St: We do....

—Also, there is something else. Reading a book also creates obstacles because, when you are reading a book, you have to follow the path taken by the author. You are living the character, you have to feel what the author came up with for him or her. The writing business is something much broader. But you are the one who is feeling your character and taking him or her along the path you want.

But when someone goes to read it, the same thing happens....

The more I read, the more complex writing becomes to me. Because the words come to my head, but, for example, when I read a novel and then have to write, I get all mixed up; I cannot write. So much so that this year I decided to go for poetry. I couldn't manage to develop a story, from reading so much; it seemed like I was somewhat incapable. It became much too complex....

Something else that happens is that when you are reading everyone has their own feelings on top of the story. And when you go to write, no matter how badly you do not want to, you end up also wanting to put the feelings that the book got across to you, or that some other reading did, into your story. That makes it complex because, when you go to write and get your feelings across, you end up picking up also some of the things you read.

The emotional aspect counts a lot; it depends on you, how you feel the book, how you are reading it. If you break the book up in many parts, the different parts you read at different times, your emotional state was different. Then, it all depends on how you piece it together.

It is really the idea of a movie that you piece together, because they give you the characters but don't give you the image. You are the one who edits the images and rolls the film in your head.

PF: What criteria do you have for finding a book or other reading enjoyable?

St: I think it is precisely the book's managing to get across to you what the author wanted.

Also, a book that hooks you....

—No, I think differently....

PF: No, I want the criteria that you have. What are the qualities? I am curious about that....

St: I think that the book really has to fit into your way....

No!

I think it has to be, above all, an engaging book. Whether a comedy or drama....

PF: Very well, then, that is one quality: any one of these books has to have a certain power of engagement....

St: Even if it is a long book....

Even if you are a person, for example, who only likes to read adventure stories and go to read a police story. The book has to be engaging no matter what.

PF: All right. Now, another quality.

St: A book could be tiring for one person and not for another; it depends on the person....

To one person it could be tiring, and to another it could not be. I think the criteria vary a lot from person to person.

PF: No, but I want to know the criteria you have here.

St: It also depends on the moment.

That is what I think. For example, it might be that I read a novel ten years ago (ten years ago can't be, say, about three years ago) that I wanted to read then and no longer do today; that is, it depends on the moment....

—It depends on each person....

PF: I know, but look, in your moment of today, what is it that a book must have in order for you to say, "Wow, this book is enjoyable"?

St: I am going through a phase where I feel like reading novels.

PF: Great, then. You read novels.

St: But two months ago I felt like reading science fiction. I love it. I can read everything, but right now, I am more open to reading novels.

PF: Well, then, what must novels have for you to say, "Wow, this novel is enjoyable"?

St: I think it is whether it creates, or gets across, an illusive image to me. I am more for a novel that ends well than one that ends badly, right?

PF: That's great.

St: (laughter) That's it....

PF: Hey, do you guys realize that I am sixty-seven years old, and I continue to, I mean, "I am more for that, too."

St: (laughter)

I read a novel just now that ended badly, so I cried an entire afternoon (laughter). But, at the same time, it was good....

—The book ends up becoming part of the reader, right?

PF: But tell me another quality.

St: Another?

At the same time you get mad at a book, sometimes.

PF: Oh, that is good, right? (laughter)

St: I think so, too.

—The book is good to a point that it even manages to provoke you.

The book is good when it manages to move you. It is not enough to just get across what the guy is thinking, but it has to know how to get it across while moving you.

Yeah, it has to provoke the reader.

A book is also very good, as you keep reading it, to get you started thinking about a bunch of things.

Sometimes you are reading, and you identify with some character. And that is when you realize what you are good at, whether you are a cool person, and at what you are not, you know what I mean? Then you stop and think, "Hold on. I do that." That is what happens to you the most.

There is also something beautiful, which is the topic you are interested in. For example, if you want to learn. You can look at an encyclopedia. If you are interested in World War II, you will start out reading, for example, *A bicicleta azul, Olga, O sétimo segredo,* everything about Hitler, and then you will also want to understand what communism is, socialism. After that, you become interested in the human body, so you go to read a scientific book, which is also something that can keep your interest...

Right, it is not like reading an encyclopedia....

It is important, for example, for you to do it like this: take a book that you read three years ago, and then you will read that book again...

It is a different thing....

Totally....

... and in ten or five years, you will have a completely different view on that book.

Many times you relate a book to yourself.

You relate the book not only to yourself, to your feelings, but also with what is around you.

Yes, to life, right?

I think a book can open up different paths for you in other subjects or even in subjects you are tired of reading about.

I think that a good book is one that reaches your life, interacts with your life.

But, in the same way, I believe the following: When you reread a book, it is not like your head has changed; it is not that what took place was wrong; it is just that at that moment you picked up on a part of the message you were inclined to pick up on.

—I think what a book says is never wrong. Nothing is ever wrong. . . .

PF: Now, I would like to ask another question with respect to that. How about from the standpoint of the author's language? What touches you?

St: Language that is closer to our own. . . .

St: No, I prefer more poetic language.

St: Language that has to do with the book, for example, if the language is southern. . . .

St: That is true.

St: Not language completely different from the moment where the book lives. For example, if the book takes place during World War II with language from the future, that will have nothing to do with the book. And with the language that was there, you will become more engaged in the book.

PF: That means, then, that the language is historic?

St: Yes, the language also agrees with the book.

Books that bring tiring language, that is, if you cannot stay with it, it will be the hardest thing for you to stay engaged in the book because reading it will tire you out.

I think something else. For example, I was reading *Macunaíma,* and it was something, like there were tons of words that I could not understand at all! Then, since I wanted to understand everything, I became more involved in the book. Because it was language that had nothing to do with anything; that it was really *Macunaíma*'s way; it had nothing to do with me, but it was language that makes you become engaged; you want to get it. It is like a challenge.

Which has to do with the book, right?

There is interest and lack of interest; it depends on the person.

Another thing. I read *A cor púrpura* [*The Color Purple*] and through her language, the main character's, it was possible to understand; it got a lot more across to me than just my imagination. Also through imagination, but through the language I was able to imagine much better things, and different things, too.

A cor púrpura has language that is not as grammatical as the teacher's language.

PF: Now, I would like to ask a few questions related to the reading, but from the standpoint, now, of the reader, not from the standpoint of the text. In other words, I asked from the standpoint of the text, what you guys thought about it, what the qualities are for you of a text, and we already measured it. Now I would like to ask you what qualities the reader must have, including noticing the qualities of the text.

St: One must be willing to read....I think that the person must pick up the book with an open mind to see what it is saying....

One has to be willing to do that; if you pick up a book not willing to read anything, you really can't understand it.

PF: Very well. What does it mean to "pick up a book with an open mind"?

St: It means that you are willing to learn.

Being willing to receive different things.

PF: That's it.

St: You have to be willing to receive other things, rather than just keep your own opinion.

PF: Then, just making a parenthesis here, would you notice how writing and reading require, in fact, freedom. You see, I recognize that there are times when I don't feel like reading. I recognize that there are times when I do not feel like writing. But, as a function of my duty, irrespectively of whether I feel like it or not, I read. For example, just a moment ago I was not feeling like reading, and I am reading a three-hundred-page dissertation. Why? Let me explain it to you. Because I am a professor at a university, and one of my duties as a university professor, or when I am called upon (and, of course, I am not obligated) to integrate a doctoral dissertation committee, or master's, or another degree doesn't matter, I have the duty to accept it and to participate. And, for that reason, I have to read the person's dissertation because I cannot question someone without reading.

St: No, but I think that, if you feel like reading, if someday you were to pick up this dissertation while feeling like reading, I think it would be different....

PF: Hold on, hold on. Let us not turn reading exclusively into pleasure. Sometimes, reading can even start out with a bit of pain, and it is that point of pain, to me, that will bring about in me the taste for having overcome the pain.

St: But even then. Even with a reading you do not particularly like, it can at some point, depending on what part you receive, be productive.

PF: It can be, and we have to make it so. So that is what I want to say. Because an irresponsible teacher, for example, now when you guys said, "Oh, there are times when we are not up for reading," might say, "Oh, well, then, you are right. If you are not up for reading, don't read—the heck with that teacher." No way! And a responsible teacher cannot do that.

St: Then, someone who does not feel like reading will never read....

PF: They never would read. Now, of course, you will have moments when you are you and times when you continue to be yourself but with a different task. One thing is when you, because you like it, because you want to, because you have a yearning for it, pick up your novel and read it. Another thing is when you have a task that is fundamental for your education, even if it is a drag, but you will discover it to be important tomorrow, the task of reading a book. You will just have to read it. I mean, if you do not read it, you become irresponsible from the standpoint of a necessary obligation. Now, ideally (but we don't live ideally), you would join both things together. I find it wonderful! When I wrote this piece that you read, I found it to be wonderful because I was enjoying that I was writing, and I was completing a task as well. And I thought it was great that I was preparing a speech for a conference.

St: Oh, I too think it is not like that, just to wait around: "Oh, I feel like it; I don't feel like it...."

One needs to know how to transform oneself in order to pick up that book....

It is not just like getting yourself a book whether you want to read or not. But you keep on reading, and you end up enjoying the book because it is a cool book for you to read, because it is your time to read it.

In the beginning you said that reading was about being open to receive new things and to transform that. So, that is it; even if you do not feel like it, you have to be open to reading and to realizing it was good. And you really had to read to notice that.

Even if you do not like it, as an experience, you finish the book because it will bring you some benefit. I think you have to locate well what you did not like, why you did not like it.

PF: That's right....

St: So, another thing is that you become much more open to the various subjects you are reading about. Then you become better able to distinguish better the books you like from those you do not.

Many personal experiences come into play as well; it is not just the book you are reading that brings experiences.

But I agree that it has to be a book about something you like. Because I think the issue is for you to look for the type of book you want to read.

I think you have to read a little of what you like because, when you do not like something, you will have to know why...

No, you have to separate the two readings. You have your assignment for school, which is a handout, and there is no getting away from it; you have to read it. It may be tomorrow or the day after, but you have to read it. Now, when you choose what you are going to read, it is a different kind of literature; it is different from an assignment. Then, I think it is up to you to choose; it is your choice. You can finish it or not.

(All speaking at once)

St: Even when I chat with myself, even when I feel like reading a school handout, or a book, even if it was not assigned, when I pick it up to read it, it is always a challenge to me to get past the first page, to concentrate. Once we have concentrated, books open up. I end up getting involved, for example, in a social studies handout, or some other book. In the end, I do get involved. I think, even in relation to the books I do want to read, it is always hard to get started at the beginning, because it is always hard for you to disconnect from certain things....

PF: Look, there are certain things that, in order to read, we must avoid, to read well, to read seriously. It is like some sort of demons or devils that interfere with our reading, with our need to fixate on the reading. You should experiment with that as well. Sometimes, we are reading a page, and all of a sudden, we leave; we remain with our bodies in the chair, next to the desk, with the book in front of us, and from that point on, we read mechanically. We keep on mechanically reading the text, and we displace ourselves; the other part of us comes out of us and, suddenly, we are in a pool, chatting with this or that friend, at the movies. In other words, those escapes from the reading pose a complete obstacle to our understanding. Either we engage in the exercise of not escaping, or we lose the reading. That is an indication that there is some lack of interest on our part. Then, my suggestion for when that happens is: It is better to stop reading and ask ourselves why there is no motivation for reading. Something else I would like to suggest to you is that, every time you are reading a book, some text, and you do not understand the meaning of a word, do not wait for that word to come up again to see if after it comes up many times you will end up getting what it means. Consult a dictionary. That is what dictionaries exist for. Go and get the dictionary, look up the word and see what the word means. Now, it is 12:00 noon, and I wanted to say just two things to you. The first one is that I came here today precisely due to that issue of duty and conscience. It is just that I had a not-so-great night. I allowed myself a few excesses, and I paid a little, not too much, but I did pay some. I had too much shrimp and all that stuff....

St: (laughter)

It is gluttony, right?

PF: Yes, gluttony. I ended up with a pain in my big toe. You will know what that means.... Then, I had a bad night, and now this morning, as I came here, I was a bit distant. I know when I am not well. You may possibly have noticed that I was not well. I couldn't even talk, chat.... But I came anyway. That is, I thought that it would have been terrible to call here and say, "Tell the boys and girls that I could not come because I was not feeling well." I thought that would have been disrespectful toward you and toward the school. I had proposed this and had accepted this invitation.... So, then, I had a bit of a struggle with myself. And the rest of the struggle is that I feel fine now. I mean, I have recovered and feel excellent. I don't know if I'll be able to handle the afternoon. I am traveling to Recife today, so I don't even know if I will be teaching. But I was happy. These forty minutes I spent here with you were absolutely great. The second thing that I would like to say is the following: What just happened here is school, or rather, it is a part, or it is a hypothesis of the school I dream of for the people of Brazil.

St: (laughter)

PF: The sad part is that the example you provided me today is an example of beautifulness, but one that awakens in me an unfulfilled desire: I found this morning to be a beautiful thing, a group of young people, boys and girls, thinking, thinking without fear, putting out ideas, meditating, analyzing themselves, asking questions, giving intelligent, emotive opinions.... In other words (*wow!*), this gives me great happiness as a Brazilian. Now, what I really wanted was for this to be also for popular masses, that is, for the popular classes, for the kids in the stream.... That is why I am for a good public school, but I also respect the good private school. I want to congratulate you, congratulate your teachers, the management of the house, for today I believe I had one of those good mornings, which I had not had in a long time, and to me that is a thing of beauty. Since I feel just about your age....

St: (laughter)

PF: —even though I am not, chronologically, I was extremely glad because I felt like I was among fellows of mine; do you know what I mean? Because I am twenty years old; I am eighteen; I am fifteen, in spite of the sixty-seven years and foot pains.

St: (laughter)

PF: OK, so I want you all to feel hugged by me, everyone here, without any exception; I send you all a big kiss as well. Keep up the good work; after all, Brazil belongs to you, rather than to that shameless crowd that is out there to ruin the country. See you soon, huh?

ENDNOTES

1. A dialogue that took place on October 20, 1988, between Paulo Freire and the students in the seventh and eighth grades at Escola Vera Cruz in São Paulo. Transcribed by Cristina Chiappini Moraes Leite, originally published in *Linha D'Agua* magazine (1988), no. 6.

6

HUMAN RIGHTS AND LIBERATING EDUCATION[1]

↤

When I came in, the back way I believe, and looked at this lecture hall trying to see it in its totality, fully packed, I almost thanked God when I was told to go to the teachers' lounge and wait there for ten to fifteen minutes, while more people were possibly arriving. And I, who was thinking about starting, enjoyed going to the teachers' lounge, and even pedagogically, I must say, above all to the young people here but also to the less young: I welcomed that interruption as it gave me the opportunity to compose myself some, and to recover from a certain fear of speaking that came over me today.

Speaking about this fear is pedagogical, especially to the young, because as I explain it, I might lose some humility—it is pedagogical because the young need to know that older men, sometimes more or less known men, men used to speaking, writing, and giving interviews, used to coordinating conferences in and out of their own country, can also, at times, become shy before an audience.

It just so happens that people like me have gained a certain experience in speaking, taming one's feelings, and fooling fear when necessary. One of such tactics for fooling fear is, precisely, to say that one has fear.

While I was recovering from that legitimate fear, I was thinking that I have the right also to experience fear, to be shy, to ask myself: Could it be that I can indeed say something worthwhile? Something that makes sense? That fear was made to increase when I was told that this lecture would become a book. One of the things that horrifies me the most is to read myself after I have been recorded. It is work I do not enjoy a great deal but that needs to be done.

The topic that was assigned to me is Education and Human Rights: Liberating Education. I shall put some questions to myself with respect to that.

The first question I put to myself is that of how speaking about Education and Human Rights already presents us with a first right denied and being denied, which is the right to an education. It is education itself that we intend to go to the effort of challenging those who prohibit education from being made; it is education itself as a right of all that is denied to a large part of the population. And this first reflection immediately leads me to the realization of another obviousness, which is precisely the political nature of education, that is, the realization of the absolute impossibility of having an educative process that is oriented toward the "well-being of humanity," for example. As I say that, I remember my youth, my reading of a few naive philosophy-of-education books that tried to explain or define education as being an effort at the service of humanity or of humanity's well-being. That does not in fact happen or exist. The impossibility of education's neutrality results from this quality education possesses of being political, not necessarily partisan, obviously.

Such politicalness of education comes to the fore, indeed, the moment we think about Education and Human Rights. We don't even need to try to define what we understand by human rights, but the very moment we think about education and human rights, basic rights, the right to eat, the right to dress, the right to sleep, the right to have a pillow and to rest one's head on it at night, for that is one of the central rights of the so-called *human animal,* the right to rest, to think, to ask oneself, to walk, the right to loneliness, the right to communion, the right to be *with,* the right to be *against,* the right to fight, to speak, to read, to write, the right to dream, the right to love. I believe those to be fundamental rights, and for that very reason, I started out with the right to eat, to dress, to be alive, the right to decide, the right to work, to be respected, when we think and realize the political nature of education to be this thing that makes education unviable as a neutral practice. This thing requires, demands from educators, not mattering whether they are criminal law professors or preschool teachers. It does not matter whether it is a postgraduate philosophy of education professor, or a biology, or math, or physics teacher.

The political nature of education vehemently demands that teachers take a stand for themselves as political beings, that they discover themselves in the world as political beings, rather than as mere technicians or persons of knowledge, because they too, technicians and persons of knowledge, are substantively political. The politicalness of education requires that a teacher know him/herself, in objective terms and on an objective level, on the level of his or her practice, *in favor* of someone or *against* someone, *in favor* of some dream and, therefore, *against* a certain societal scheme, a certain project of society. That is why, then, the political nature of education requires that the educator see him/herself within objective practice as a participant *in favor of* or *against* someone or something. This politicalness requires that the educator be coherent about that choice.

In that sense, a teacher has the right to be reactionary, as his or her choice may be toward the stabilization of the status quo. The reactionary teacher is absolutely convinced that things as they are out there are excellent. Evidently, everything is excellent, I agree, for a certain type of people, including this hypothetic teacher I am speaking about now. Fortunately, the majority of Brazilian teachers are on a different wavelength. But the reactionary teacher has to be coherent, in his or her reactionary choice, toward his or her ideological position. Therefore, obviously, to this teacher the phrase Education and Human Rights sounds quite distinct from what the same phrase sounds like to me. To the reactionary teacher,

Education and Human Rights has to do with educating the dominant class, fighting to preserve the material conditions of the society that is out there, so that the dominant class, while reproducing its ideology and its power through education, may preserve its political and economic power in power.

In order to be consistent with his or her political choice in his or her practice, this teacher must, first of all, be a competent teacher. Incidentally, to make a parenthesis, I would say that is possibly the only coincidence between the two, progressive and reactionary teachers; both have to be competent; both have to teach for real.

From that point on, the manner in which they teach cannot be the same. That brings us to the issue of the relationship between method, content, and objective, which is a philosophical discussion in nature, but also a political one, and a fundamental one to me, from the standpoint of the educator's education. The nonviability of the dichotomy between content, methods, and objectives, for example—that is, my dream has to do with content and the methods for addressing that content: I cannot address the same content in the same manner as a reactionary teacher does. I do not mean to say that, to a reactionary math teacher, for example, four times four might be fifteen, given that in a decimal system it is always sixteen. But there are a number of implications in that four times four equals sixteen that have to do with the teacher's political-ideological stances, which we should not go into here.

But the same phrase, the same theme, Education and Human Rights, sounds differently according to the teacher's political, ideological outlook. By saying that it is as if I were, in some way, hurting that fantastic dream of all these young intellectuals who work and who lead this whole movement, as they throw themselves into a fantastic campaign on Education and Human Rights. No. What I say does not in any way diminish the need for that project to be put into practice. I, too, believe in it.

All I mean to say is that there will be different intelligences about this project, which can be explained in light of the political choices of educators. While to an elitist teacher, for example, Education in Human Rights has to do with the lofty treatment of knowledge, that is, treating the act of discovering in a lofty manner. To a progressive teacher the discussion about the act of gaining knowledge presents itself more as a right of men and women from the popular classes, who have been precluded from exercising that right, the right to better know what they already know because they practice it, and the right to participate in the creation of knowledge that does not yet exist.

While an elitist teacher orients education as some sort of curbing for the popular classes and of growth for the representatives of the elite, a progressive educator, necessarily, cannot march to that beat. Therefore, a vision or understanding of human rights and of education depends on *how* I see myself in the world politically; it depends on who I am *with*, at *whose* service, and at the service of *what* I am an educator.

For that very reason, the problem of education, whether or not associated to human rights, since it is already a fundamental right, is not an issue that can be explained bureaucratically or pedagogically. The issue of education is understood politically, substantively. It seems to me that reflecting on that, in that way, is absolutely important and fundamental so that we do not fall into naive positions that can only frustrate and dishearten. For example, attributing to education, whether in this or any other campaign, but attributing to education the power to transform the world, sooner or later, leads all men and women marching to this drum to enormous frustration.

Yet, as I say that, it feels like I should explain, because, in fact, it is an educator who is saying it, as something obvious to me. Someone might say, then, "But why do you continue to be an educator if you have just negated education?" I would say that, first of all, I am not the one who negates education, that I am just facing up to the educative practice, historically, as it takes place. In second place, the negation to which education is exposed is the best manner it has to assert itself. What do I mean to say with such contradiction?

Education is not the key, the lever, the instrument for social transformation. It is not that, precisely because it could be it. It is precisely that contradiction that explains, that enlightens, that unveils the limited efficacy of education. What I mean to say is that education is limited; education suffers from limits. Incidentally, that is not a privilege of education, as there is no human practice that is not subjected to limits, which are historical, political, ideological, cultural, economic, social, competence limits on the part of a subject or subjects, and sanity limits; there are those limits that are part of the nature of a practice, and there are those that are implicit in the finite nature of the subjects involved in that practice.

It is exactly because education subjects itself to limits that it is effective. Let us, then, understand that contradiction: If education could be everything, and such is the naiveté of many still—I have heard from many people in this and other countries, but especially in this one, that the great problem of the country is education—as if top-down education were able to rearrange the society that is out there. Not being, it is, precisely because it is not. It is because it is not. It is because it is not that it is; because it is limited, it is effective. If education could be everything, going back to that reflection, there would be no reason to speak about its limits, as it would accomplish all. However, it is historically verified that education cannot accomplish all. Nevertheless, if it could be nothing, there would be no reason to speak about the limits of education. But it is, exactly, because while not being able to accomplish all it can accomplish "something," that the efficacy of education is to be found in that being able to accomplish something. The question put to the educator is to know what it is that education is *able to be,* which is historical, social, political.

The educator's biggest problem is not to discuss whether education can or cannot accomplish, but to discuss *where* it can, *how* it can, *with whom* it can, *when* it can; it is to recognize the limits his or her practice imposes. It is to realize that his or her work is not individual, but social, and that it takes place within the social practice he or she is a part of. It is to recognize that education, while not being the key, the lever of social transformation, as much as has been said, is nonetheless indispensable to social transformation. It is to recognize that there are possible spaces that are political, that there are institutional and extra-institutional spaces to be filled by educators whose dream is to transform the unjust reality that is out there, so that rights can start to be earned and not granted.

Education for human rights, in a perspective of justice, is precisely that education which awakens the dominated to the need for struggle, for organization, for critical, just, democratic mobilization, one serious, rigorous, disciplined, devoid of manipulations, and with a view to the reinvention of the world, to the reinvention of power. The issue being put here is not one of having educators insert themselves as a stimulus toward a taking of power that stops at the taking of power, but rather a taking of power that is extended into the reinvention of the power taken, and that is to say that such education has to do with a different understanding of development, which implies the greater and greater, growing, critical, affective participation of popular groups.

Now, I look over and see my great friend whom I have not seen or spoken with for a long time, Francisco Whitaker. I recall an excellent book of his[2] from the 1970s about development, in which he puts forth exactly a different understanding of the development process. He might criticize his book, today, a bit too harshly, and that is a good thing. I do not always criticize my previous books. But I do recall taking the manuscript of that excellent book to Africa, to write a three-page preface, as I never write more than that for a preface. I remember the immense joy in writing it, reading the book; I read it on the plane, on the trip to Africa, and when I finished, I reread the book with the smell of the African soil, with the smell of the animals of Africa, while homesick for Brazil, which was forbidden to me at the time, and Africa was like some memory of mine, it was some sort of present that I was getting, since the puritan saviors of this country, in power, would not allow a poor devil like me to return here, not even to see the ground. Africa gave itself to me like a tender, older woman who indulges a younger lover. And it was there, on that delightful ground of Africa, that culture that was mine as well, that I had the joy of writing three preface pages for Whitaker's book.

While I was speaking about that here, about this right to change the world, which goes through the right to change production, the productive act, the right to intervene in the production process, the right to say no, that is not what will be produced, the right to deny certain greedy minorities that they produce what seems right to them; that is why education associated with human rights, within this perspective that goes through an understanding of the social classes, has to do with education and liberation, rather than simply with freedom. It has to do with liberation precisely because there is no freedom, and liberation is exactly the struggle to restore or institute the joyfulness of being free that never runs out, that never ends and always begins.

It is necessary, then, that we, *educadoras*[3]—I want to say to the men present here not to doubt my virility too much, but rather agree with my ideological position of rejecting a sexist syntax that wishes to convince women that while saying "we, *educadores*, I would also be including women. I would not. And in order to prove that when I say "we, *educadores*" I am referring only to men, because I do not participate in this macho lie, I said just now, on purpose, "we, *educadoras*" in the feminine form, to provoke the men. I hope they feel incorporated to "*educadoras*" in the feminine, so they can see how bad it is. I mean how bad it is not to be a woman. How bad it is for women to be involved in a lie, in an ideology that intends to explain it syntactically as if syntax had nothing to do with ideology—a forgery.

Going back to the previous thought, I would say that it is necessary that we not allow ourselves, on the one hand, to fall into the naiveté of an all-powerful education, and on the other, into the naiveté which is to deny the potentiality of education. No. Education, while not being able to accomplish all, can accomplish something. We have the duty, politically, to find spaces for action, of organizing ourselves in those spaces. I even use, at times, language that I recognize as somewhat aggressive. I would even speak of the necessity and the wisdom we must have to invade those spaces.

Therefore, the perspective of education in human rights that we defend is this one, of a society that is less unjust, so that it can, little by little, become more just. This society must always keep on reinventing itself with a new understanding of power, going through a new understanding of production, a society in which people have a taste for living, for dreaming, for loving, for well liking. That must be a courageous, curious education, one awakening of curiosity, and for that very reason, an education that, as much as possible, keeps on preserving the girl that you were, without allowing your maturity to kill her.

I believe that one of the best things that I have done in my life, better than the books I wrote, was not to allow the boy I was not able to be, and the boy I was, to die within me. Sexagenarian, note how bad this word sounds already. I said that on purpose, just to show how history is about that. Back in my childhood, I would read a newspaper, *Diário de Pernambuco* or *Jornal do Comércio,* and they would publish, "Sexagenarian so and so passed away yesterday, and pheretrum such and such ...." Nowadays, the young generation does not know that word. They have to look it up in a dictionary. However sexagenarian, I am seven; sexagenarian, I am fifteen years old; sexagenarian, I love the ocean wave, and I love to see snow coming down; it might even seem like alienation. Some fellow leftist of mine might already be saying, "Paulo is irreversibly lost." I would say to my hypothetical leftist comrade, "I am found, precisely because I lose myself in watching the snow come down." Sexagenarian, I am twenty-five years old. Sexagenarian, I love once again and begin to create a life anew. After having lost a wife whom I loved thunderously, I begin to thunderously love once more, without any sense of guilt. Yes, that is pedagogical as well. I want to say it,

I did not actually have any reason for saying it, and I do have reasons for saying it. I would not have them, if my public criterion dichotomized my private life, but I do not dichotomize; I am a man who lives privately, publicly and publicly, privately. I am more or less the same at home and here at this college. It is then important that I say that. I have the right and the duty to say that I have married this young woman right here, who is also a girl, and whose name is Nita. I was not at all afraid of loving. And it does not seem to me that loving should require that much courage.

The education I speak about is an education of now, and it is an education of tomorrow. It is an education that must set us, permanently, on a questioning, a re-making, and an inquiring of ourselves. It is an education that does not accept, in order to be good, that it should suggest sadness to the learners. I believe in the serious and rigorous education that makes me joyous and happy. I disbelieve completely in an education that, in name of rigor, makes the world ugly. I do not believe, not in any way, in the relationship between seriousness and ugliness. As if, for example, it were necessary to write ugly in order to write rigor or rigorously. If one writes what is more beautiful, soon they'll be saying, "That is not scientific." I only write ugly when I am not capable, when I am not competent.

That education for freedom, the education linked to human rights in that perspective, has to be encompassing, totalizing; it has to do with critical knowledge of the real and with the joy of living. It does not only have to do with rigorousness of analysis on how society moves, how it progresses, gets along, but it has also to do with the feast that is life itself. Yet that has to be done in a critical rather than a naive manner. It is neither about accepting the naive all-powerfulness of an education that accomplishes all, nor about accepting the negation of education as something that accomplishes nothing, but rather about taking education with its limitations, and therefore, about doing what is possible, historically, to do *with* and *through* education, also.

Speaking some about Education and Human Rights implies that the one who speaks must also be well aware of some of his or her own rights while a speaker and while human. I will now make use of a right I have, as I apologize, in part to you all, as a matter of lovingness on my part. That is the only reason why I apologize. I will make use of the right to stop here and not to do something that characterizes me, which is to stay for an hour or two debating with the audience, regardless of its size. But it so happens that I cannot do that today. I have recovered from the fear of speaking, but I am tired, still feeling the tail end of a cold that leaves me with a terrible cough, and tomorrow I have to travel quite early to Brasília, so I must try to sleep some, to rest some from the hard day I had. So, I'll end it here and enormously thank the fantastic, beautiful, tender presence of you all, and forgive me for not joining the conversation now, in a dialogue that I would enjoy engaging in. Who knows, I might come back another night.

ENDNOTES

1. Conference held on June 2, 1988, within the Ciclo de Palestras Direitos Humanos, at the invitation of the Justice and Peace Commission of the São Paulo Archdiocese, at the Law School of the University of São Paulo (USP), at Largo de São Francisco.

2. F. W. Ferreira, *Planejamento—sim e não: um modo de agir num mundo em permanente mudança* (Rio de Janeiro: Paz e Terra, 1978).

3. Translator's note: Even though in standard Portuguese the masculine plural form, *educadores,* should be used when referring to both men and women, here the author uses the feminine form of the word, *educadoras,* to make a point about sexist language.

7

CHANGING IS DIFFICULT, BUT POSSIBLE[1]

<del>↝</del>

First of all, it would be very difficult to start my conversation today without referring to my stint here at Sesi fifty years ago. It would be not only very difficult but also unfair because the things we do and know are the product of a complexity of influences in our lives.

Unquestionably, my first work experience at Sesi, during ten years, constituted a time that inspired one of my books (*Letters to Cristina*), where I discuss that experience at Sesi, a time I call "foundation time," that is, "a time that establishes the foundation and, therefore, opens itself up to profundity." I used to discuss that with my first wife, who was to me a great educator and a great practitioner of education.... As a matter of fact, some friends say that I am the theory of Elza's practice. I think that was unfair to both of us. I had a practice as well, and she also had a theory.

Sometimes, I do not like to say something I am, as it could seem like vanity on my part, but, deep down, I am an educator who, in addition to practicing education, thinks the Theory of Education. For this reason, I am a thinker of education. I do not enjoy saying that I am a thinker of the field, because it becomes a bit aristocratic. However, in reality, that is what I have been, a thinker of education, who cannot dissociate thinking from doing. I would say to my daughter that everything I have been criticizing, discussing, questioning as an educator, as a thinker, in books, articles, conferences, discussions, seminars, everything has its roots at Sesi. That is why I call this time I lived here at Sesi—morning, afternoon, and evening—a "founder time." Back then, at the Sesi on Rio Branco Avenue [in Recife], which was open from 7:00 A.M. to 1:00 P.M., I would go back and spend the whole afternoon there, sometimes, because of some problem that had happened at one of its schools. I would think about the problem and sit there discussing it.... The interesting thing is that much of the pedagogical reading I did was on account of real problems. I think one does not simply read; it is a much more effective way of studying. In other words, I would search, in the bibliography, for the answers to a concrete fact that had taken place. Thus, I did not surrender myself randomly to theoretical reflection. That is, I sought an explanation for a concrete fact that I had lived—I would think about my practice.

I remember that in my sixteenth year in exile, a time when my name was forbidden from being published in the *Jornal do Comércio, Diário de Pernambuco,* or in the *Folha de S. Paulo*; it could not show up anywhere in the media.... How amazing! Sometimes I would become shocked at the danger I represented! I did not know that.... And I was told I was dangerous. Now, would you just think about how freedom is a threat! Curiosity toward freedom becomes a danger! I remember my friend, Heloísa Bezerra, whom I wrote constantly, from Switzerland, from the United States, long letters that she would read to a group of friends, and then, they would reply.... In other words, deep down, even in exile, my complete longing for Brazil included my experiences at Sesi.

I even told a friend a story that I will repeat here, about one of my experiences in the field of pedagogy and in the generation of humility ... because we all need to learn how to be humble. Once a month, on a Sunday, I would speak to fathers and mothers, fishermen and fisherwomen, in what we called "Parent-Teacher Circle"; I would speak, and all would keep silent. All of a sudden, I was startled by a body that tumbled to the ground. Some guy fell while sleeping. It was very hot, and it was a talk that, at some point, ended up lulling the man in such a way that he fell asleep, making a tremendous crash and "waking" all of us. That man's fall provoked in me a series of reflections, including that we never know whether we are or not reaching the people who hear us. Possibly up to that point, I may have been thinking that all that silence was an acceptance of my talk. In fact, rather than producing an instigating speech, I was singing a lullaby. I, then, criticize those classes that become lullabies in my pedagogical analyses.

In reality, then, it would be an exaggeration to say that in my ten intensely lived years at Sesi I never had a day when I did not engage in some serious reflection—that would, in reality, be an exaggeration. However, those ten years—something interesting!—were the ones when I wrote only three articles. I began to write at a quite mature age. I became noticed really in exile, not here. Now, of course, when I started to write in exile, I wrote about the great charge of the experience had here, and later that I also built in exile. In other words, I mean that stint at Sesi, and later the visits I made to other Sesi's around Brazil, the experiments made at that time, in the fifties. In Rio Grande do Sul, Mário Reis, who was superintendent, social worker, a very catholic spiritualist, very ethical, and very secure as an intellectual, conducted a good experiment. It was during my visit to Rio Grande do Sul that I met one of the best thinkers of this country, Professor Ernani Maria Fiori, a great philosopher, already passed, who wrote the preface for the Brazilian edition of *Pedagogy of the Oppressed,* which I consider to be one of the serious works about my thought and should be re-read constantly. In general, people do not read prefaces. I believe all prefaces should be read as well, especially a preface like that.

When I was invited to come here today, I confess to you that I became extremely glad, deeply touched. If I were a beginner, I would be, here and now, possibly, experiencing difficulty to speak—even for a disorganized talk such as I am giving now. But I am old enough already not to have these problems any more. Age no longer allows.... Better yet, experience is already so great that it is no longer possible to be lost.

Obviously, I do not wish to reduce my talk today to you to those delightful memories that I bring from my time at Sesi. It was not possible, however, to fail to say something about that, that is, about the dreams, the struggles to realize those dreams. I remember, for example, the beautiful struggle that took place when I dreamed that all Sesi's should, as much as possible, gain independence in relation to the Regional Department, as I was impressed at the assistencialist domination on the part of Sesi, its imperial inclination. I fought against that. At the same time, that struggle, my dialogues with the directors, with the labor leaderships from all the Sesi's, all that brought me a great many lessons, so that, years later, I could write *Pedagogy of the Oppressed*. I mean to say that my reflections on the oppressed consciousness, about the present of the oppressed, and the dominant depth of the dominator, about the possibility, for the oppressed, of adapting so as to survive, all that I learned here, and I confirmed it later in my experiences in Africa and Latin America.

But I remember my struggle, my dialogue, and how I lost myself, when I proposed, for example, to Sesi members that they should, through dialogue with the department directorships, move toward charging for services provided and that part of that revenue should stay at the clubs and part should go to the Regional Department, which would reinvest in more services. I remember that one fellow Sesi member, a leader, and a laborer then, stood up and gave a speech where he said, with great force, "The noble superintendent—*they called me that a lot*—is an enemy of work and a friend of capital. He is against work and in favor of capital." Days later, I was called in by a Sesi council member, who told me that I was a friend of work and an enemy of capital. I should not say here who that fellow was. It is not necessary. Nobody asked. And even if anyone does, I will not say. But it suffices to note how they took notice of that, how they questioned me.... What did that council member really mean to say, when he called me into his office? It was a difficult relationship. What was indeed behind his discourse? Was there or not some ideology? What is an ideology?

All that was extremely useful to me. Just so you can have an idea, I wrote *Pedagogy of the Oppressed,* the first three chapters, in fifteen days. The fourth chapter gave me the most work; I spent a month on it.... But I had such a degree of lived experience with the theme that it all came out just as it is in the book ... Sometimes I feel like making a *sui generis* reading of the book, highlighting pages and indicating, for example, what this had to do with the conversations I had at Sesi in such a year... In other words, I would map out the entire context of the book and the greater context, which were my experiences, including those from here; that is, some things that to this day still sometimes emerge in my reflections. Many things I lived through back then I did not come to realize until much later, or years later, like today; I am able to recognize the afternoon when, while talking to somebody in my office, I had a *spark* with respect to that theoretical reflection I am engaging in now. I have always said that in the book *Letters to*

Cristina I dedicate an entire letter to Sesi.... I believe I provide some theoretical reconstructions and make explicit exactly how much I learned here.

I could not fail to speak about this affection that even moves me to emotion, this gratitude.... It does not matter whether I agree or disagree with Sesi's political perspectives; it does not matter, for example, that I do not accept a present tendency, not only at Sesi Pernambuco, but at all Sesi's, which has been termed, incorrectly, "modernity." Modernity, my foot! In reality it is some bad postmodernity, as it is about transforming the organism and the affective relations that take place within it into business-bureaucratic hardness, that is, a search for company-like efficacy. I believe that we can be efficacious without becoming a drag, without hurting others. It does not matter what position I hold with respect to Sesi, or what position Sesi might hold about me; what matters is that Sesi was important in my philosophical education, in my political-pedagogical education, or it had an undeniable importance. In other words, Sesi made a number of things viable that were absolutely necessary to my education as an educator.

Now it is up to me, at the end of this program for your permanent education, to say something to you that I hope will not take too much time, and that is, on the one hand, to underscore the importance of permanent educational or educative experiences and, on the other, underscore something that at times we forget, and that is contained in this sentence: "Changing is difficult, but it is possible."

I think there has never been a greater need for this sentence than there is today, in Brazil. I can also say that about a month and a half ago I delivered a book to the publishers, where one of the topics I discuss is this one. The book will be called *Pedagogy of Freedom: Ethics, Democracy, and Civic Courage*. This is a book where I was concerned with analyzing certain types of knowing that I consider particularly indispensable to any educator, obviously with nuances, as a function of whether the educator is progressive or conservative. And one such knowing that I explain is exactly this one: "Changing is difficult, but it is possible."

I want to say this to you because, if I were not absolutely convinced of the truth in that statement, I would not be here right now. Obviously, from the standpoint of what it means humanly to me to be here with you, I would be, irrespectively of anything else. But, if there were not this greater foundation, which is my affective link to this organization, and not necessarily to each of you personally—I may actually not even know you—I would not have to be here. Furthermore, I would have no business being a teacher if I were not absolutely certain that changing is difficult, but it is possible.

I felt extremely happy, recently, when one of the people responsible for a sector of this institution told me that her father, eighty years of age today, was, back in my day, a Sesi janitor. And when this person told her father that she was going to talk to me, he told her, "Listen to what Prof. Paulo is going to say; clearly say what you want, and observe that, when he speaks again, he will make you convinced that you know. One of Paulo Freire's characteristics is that, while talking to someone, he will insist on making it clear that the person with whom he speaks also knows."

She understood how worthwhile that appreciation on the part of her father was to him! I told her, "Deep down, your father was making a theoretical synthesis of the educator Paulo Freire's thought." That is, my comprehension of the process of knowing, the production of knowledge, my *trekkings around* through what is being called, today, constructivism.... I am even the father of constructivism. There isn't any doubt that it is not possible to study constructivism, in this country, without speaking of me—and even out of this country.... You see, I loathe false modesty. If I were not absolutely convinced that I had something to say here, I would not have accepted the invitation. Now, in having accepted the invitation, I would not come here to say that another should have been here.... In that case, better not to have come.... I loathe that. If I come here, it is because I think I can. Now, modesty lies not in doubting who should be here; modesty lies in knowing that there are others who could also be. Yes to that. It is actually possible that others might do it a bit better than myself—there is no doubt. Now, denying that I too can do it is what I think is false, hypocritical—I am not fond of hypocrisy. But for that very reason I accept this constructivism issue, which the superintendent mentioned in his talk. In other words, he made reference to the emphasis I give to the circumstance, to the knowing, or to the experiences of the learner. That is one of the fundamental principles of constructivism, which has in Piaget its great leader.

But as I was saying to that person, "Your father makes a synthesis of the theoretical effort...." You see, he participated in some of the meetings, while a janitor, a young man, not in courses, but he picked up exactly on the fundamental spirit of what I propose, which is the capacity for being the subject in the production of one's own knowledge. Years later, maybe thirty or forty years later, he brings that up as his own discourse. And I told her, "You see how this expression on the part of your father shows, on the one hand, the limitations and, on the other, the possibilities of education."

Therefore, education is that. Maybe one of the best ways for conceiving of education is to say that it cannot accomplish it all, but it can accomplish something. That is, our problem, of educators, is to ask ourselves if it is possible to make viable what sometimes does not seem possible.

I go back, then, to insisting on this sentence: "Changing is difficult, but it is possible." I would also like to add some two or three rules, above all, with respect to why the impossibility of change seems impossible to me.

First of all, I would say that the possibility alone of saying that it is impossible makes possible the impossible. Let me try to explain this—it came out too abstract. What I mean to say is the following: Only the beings that have become, through their long experience in the world, able to signify the world are capable of changing the world and are incapable of not changing. And those beings are precisely men and women. Among all living beings, we have been, thus far, the competent ones. For that very reason, more than having a history, we make our own history. See, for example, that we tell the history of lions. The lions have history, but they do not have historicity. In other words, lions do not know themselves as making history. The history of lions is told not by lions themselves, but by us. For that reason, as well, one cannot speak of the ethics of lions. It was not recorded, in the history of humanity, that African lions had murdered two fellow lions from another family group and that, at night, they had gone to the family of the dead to pay their respects, etc. This type of malefaction only men and women can commit! Only beings that *ethicize* the world are capable of rupturing with ethics. Only beings capable of fine things, of great gestures, are capable of horrid things. Thus, the *ethicization* of the world engenders the violation of ethics. And, at the same time that it engenders the violation of ethics, it requires a struggle on our part in favor of ethics.

That is what is missing today! Not only that, but that is one of the flaws in Brazil, today. That is, we lack precisely ethical rigorousness, which we should be struggling for! The democratization of faulty ethics in the country is such that no one takes anyone seriously any longer. Everyday new scandals are aired in this country's public and private life. However, not all that is said in this country can end up without any consequence. It is truly scandalous what is taking place in this country! There are no more limits! At some point in the contravention of ethics, necessarily, impunity sets in! In other words, impunity is a necessity for the advancement of

ethical violations. Impunity in Brazil is something amazing! And the more impunity there is, the greater is the
degree of ethics violation. If there were accountability,
there'd be a decrease in shamelessness. One of the great-
est democratizations in Brazil is that of shamelessness.
There is a famine of shame! Shamelessness has become
generalized!

Thus, at a moment like this, there is an ideological
tendency to say, "That is the reality of things," "Such is
reality indeed." For example, there is much talk about
unemployment, not only in Brazil, but unemployment
in the world. The world is closing the century and the
millennium with an astronomical quantity of unemployed
people! And we hear in response that "that is the reality
of things." It is not! That is not the reality of things.
There is no reality that is because it has to be. Reality
can and must be mutable; it must be transformable.
However, in order to justify the interests that pose obstacle to change, it is necessary to say "that's the way
things are." The discourse of impossibility, therefore,
is an ideological and reactionary discourse. In order to
confront the ideological discourse of impossibility of
change, it is necessary to create an equally ideological
discourse for the possibility of change, but one also
founded in the scientific truth that it is possible to
change. I do not accept; I refuse completely this profoundly pessimistic statement that it is not possible to
change. I think, as a matter of fact, that the discourse
of world change impossibility—and here lies some of
what is tragic about this discourse—is not a discourse
that can be verified.

The impossibility of changing is not something obvi-ous. For example, something obvious about Saturdays is that they precede Sundays. If the impossibility of change were as obvious as the fact that Saturdays pre-cede Sundays, I confess to you that I would not have any interest in continuing to be alive. In other words, if being a man or a woman were to put me as something obvious, impossible to change, I would prefer not to be a man or a woman; I would sooner not continue in the world. I like being human because I live between the possibility of changing and the difficulty of chang-ing. It is living the dialectic of being able to and not being able to that satisfies my presence in the world, of a being that, at the same time—and for that reason—is the object of history, and once self-recognized as such, can come to be the subject of history. That is, it is this possibility of surpassing the condition of object and reaching the condition of subject, maker of the world, remaker of the world, that nurtures me at seventy-five. I confess to you that I would have no interest—not any whatsoever—in continuing in the world if continuing in the world meant, to me, not being able to write about this. What would I be, then? A shadow in the world?

At the same time, the moment I become a maker of the possibility discourse, just making the possibility dis-course is already proof of impossibility. Therefore, I could not be, and that is why we are not determined—that is the great difference: we are conditioned. Conditioned subjects overcome the conditioning power, while de-termined subjects become enslaved to the determinant power. In other words, it is only the animals which are beings that are not able to gain consciousness of themselves once they gain consciousness of the world—thus change would be impossible. Thusly, those beings would not even be able to speak about not changing or about changing, for they would not have the language to say it. The moment we invent a language, and the social production of that language, changing is possible. Evidently, change is subjected to difficulties. There is no doubt about that. That is, change is not arbitrary; you do not change because you want to, nor do you always change in the direction you dream of. What is necessary to know is that change is not individual; it is social, with an individual dimension. But change is possible!

In closing—after all, I spoke for fifteen minutes about my reminiscences, and I do not regret it—I would say that the role of education is of enormous importance. There was a time when it was thought that education could accomplish it all, and there was a time when it was thought that education could not accomplish anything. I believe the great value of education lies in that, while not having it all, it can accomplish a lot. Thus, one of our tasks, as educators, is exactly to reflect on what is possible. And what is possible is historically, socially, and ideologically conditioned as well. What is possible, for example, in Recife today is not necessarily so in Caruaru, and vice versa. I mean, it is necessary to uncover, after all, the historic, social, political, and other conditioning, within which possibilities either take place or do not take place. Simply diagnosing those possibilities is an enormous task for the educator, along with other professionals.

I would like, therefore, to share with you a soul full of hope. To me, without hope there is no way we can even start thinking about education. In fact, the matrixes of hope are matrixes of the very *educability* of beings, of human beings. It is not possible to be unfinished beings, such as we are, conscious of that inconclusiveness, and not seek. Education is precisely that seeking movement, that permanent search.

I believe the programs, the educative gatherings where problems such as that are studied are fundamental gatherings, which help us to keep on confronting obstacles. To that end, however, it is necessary not to allow hope to run out, and the existence of the struggle to run out. I say to you, precisely because of something more profound where I root my pedagogical and political convictions: at seventy-five years of age, I possess more strength to fight, not from the physical standpoint, but from the intellectual, the moral standpoint, than I did at twenty-five—exactly when I was here, at Sesi, starting out.... It is just that I do not accept that my hope could run out. I fight; I struggle daily. Today—everything seems to indicate—I am, in a number of aspects, a younger man than when I was forty years old. When I was forty years old, or thirty-five, or thirty, and I was a teacher here, at the university, I would teach class in a suit and tie, and I never went around dressed as I showed up here, today. In other words, today, at seventy-five, I dress more modernly than when I was thirty. I am younger at seventy-five than when I was forty! I hope that in another ten years I am younger still than today....

That is what is important for us to hold on to, important for us to keep. In spite of everything, in spite of any failure! We must even know that failures or suffering are part of the search for efficacy. There is no efficacy that does not trip up on bumps toward success. It is necessary to work through failures and turn them into accomplishment.

ENDNOTE

1. Conference held in February 1997, in Recife (PE), an event organized by Serviço Nacional da Indústria (Sesi). A sinoptic version of this conference was published by Confederação Nacional da Indústria (CNI) and by SESI in homage to Paulo Freire after his passing.

8

DIALOGUE WITH THE PARTICIPANTS:
THE READING AND WRITING ISSUE

⟿

Liking or not liking to read has a lot to do with our own intellectual history. I have no doubt that it is not only school that is responsible for that, but one of the tasks of school should be exactly to encourage and challenge a taste for reading. And school does not always do that. At the same time, Brazil—not only Brazil, but I am citing our case—has lived an experience somewhat dramatic. Before overcoming difficulties with people who have not gained reading experience, Brazil intensified visual communication through television. That is, television arrived in Brazil when we had not yet had reading. We have a culture, in certain centers, that is predominantly oral, while in other centers there is an oral culture—not predominantly, but oral.

Just so you can have an idea, in 1968, the celebrated year of youth uprising in the world, I was exiled in Chile and was called to Paris by UNESCO. I went, then, to Paris in the month of June 1968, that is, one month after all that had broken out—it was May. So I got to Paris in June; the uprising in Paris and in the rest of the world had happened in May—and it was still going on—and I bought twenty-five works about May (a few pamphlets, books, others) that dealt with the phenomenon of a month earlier. That is the experience of a written culture! The experiences that were had here in this fantastic city of Recife, before the coup, have not yet been written out. For example, how many fundamental books do we have about MCP[1] in Brazil, in Pernambuco? We do not have three; maybe there are not two. We have essays—I myself have written.... One of the letters in the book *Letters to Cristina* is about MCP.... Anyway, in Paris, in the month of June 1968, I bought twenty-five books on the events of the month of May of the same year. We are in 1997, and we do not have three books about one of the most serious things that the history of this country's popular culture has, which is and which was MCP. There is no doubt that MCP was a revolutionary proposition, a conscious, strong, memorable one.... And there is nothing on it! Not even us, those who founded it.... We are going to die; a few have already died.

Germano Coelho is out there. I sent him a message telling him that I hope he will give up this habit of being mayor.... There is, here, no disrespect for him or for being mayor, but I think that what we expect from Germano Coelho is that he lock himself up in his library and write, for a year, about his political-pedagogical experience. And that he get to be mayor as well, but that he tell what MCP was. May Paulo Rosas write about MCP; may Anita Paes Barreto, one of the most serious woman intellectuals and scientists that, not only Recife, but this country has, do it as well! As a matter of fact, in São Paulo, I look for people interested in recording memories.... We have no memory! ... And one of the characteristics of our culture is exactly a more oral memory, that we do not record.

Just so you have an idea of the degree to which ours is an oral culture, I am considered, among other Brazilian intellectuals, to be one that writes *best sellers*—books that sell more. Do you know the number of copies in a normal printing for a youngster who starts publishing, here in São Paulo? Three thousand copies. In other words, an individual who sells three thousand books in a year, in São Paulo, is considered a great book seller! Brazil does not buy many books, nor does it sell many books, or read many books.

And another argument as to not reading is that the salaries of teachers in this country are absolutely not viable. To make what we make! ... I include myself in that. I am an intellectual, an atypical teacher, in Brazil, since I have other things—I sell books, write, I travel, participate in conferences in Brazil and out of Brazil.... That means money as well. Now, try to imagine an individual who makes four hundred, five hundred *reais* (plural of the Brazilian currency, the *real*) going around buying books!? I mean, the fewer books someone buys, the less he or she will like reading! And, certainly, it even becomes a defense of his [or her] not to read!

Look, the issue of reading by teachers is a matter of cultural policy, in this country, and a very complex one, indeed a serious one, requiring not only criticism of teachers. The ideal situation would be if all could read something, but that is not always possible.

However, if you [addressing the superintendent of Sesi Pernambuco] ask me whether I am completely pessimistic, I will tell you I am not. I believe that the teaching profession, in this country, has something magical, at times. For example, how else could you explain that a man like you has had an entire life dedicated to it? If you had oriented your intelligence and your ability to live, to handle the world seriously, toward something else, you would have made a lot more. Nevertheless, you stayed and remain here—and I do not expect you to leave.... That is also my case, as it is everybody's case here. In other words, there is something there.... I'm not going to tell you it is a vocation, like a religious calling, as I do not think that to be the case. This business of a calling, I think, is about tricking us into not going on strike. In reality, this country owes a great deal to the so-called lay teachers, who buy, out of the fifteen *reais* they make a month—sometimes they make a little bit more—the chalk that the city or the state does not supply. I think we should, at the closing of every pedagogical meeting, pay homage to the teachers of this country, not the academicians, but above all, those who are down and out, with their minimum wages.... Now, as you see, there is even a proposal by someone from Paraiba for different salaries! What a horrible thing! I was profoundly offended, yesterday, when I heard about two salaries. The most "wicked" salary is for public servants, teachers....

THE LIMITS AND POSSIBILITIES OF EDUCATION

When we reflect on the limits of education and the possibilities of education, it is necessary to be careful not to exaggerate on the positive and not to exaggerate on the negative, or in other words, not exaggerate on impossibility and not to exaggerate on possibility. That is, education cannot accomplish it all, but education can accomplish something and should be thought through with great seriousness by society. I believe that civil society and all of us really need to fight—to fight for seriousness in public school, for example. My issue is not fighting against the private school, whose history in Brazil has a fundamental and important presence, but rather fighting for the duty the state has to offer a serious school, to offer schooling in quantity and quality. It is not the state's role to come up here and say, "You cannot build a school; that is my duty, my right." No! Quite the contrary, the state should cooperate with private institutions that make their contribution, with private schools that make a contribution, but it cannot fail to fulfill its duty, which is to provide a serious school, a democratic school, an open school, and one where the learner experiences the possibilities that education offers and recognizes the limits of education itself.

This has been one of the reasons for my fighting as a Brazilian educator, and one of the reasons for my struggle—and, I repeat, I learned a great deal from that fight—when I directed what was called, at the time, Divisão de Educação e Cultura do Sesi. Here I learned the need for educating, internally, teachers, for respecting the freedom of learners, and the growth of learners. However, I mean a freedom that is only legitimized when it takes responsibility for its own limits! There is no freedom without limits!

I think that sometimes we exaggerate a lot our comprehension of needy children. It is as if we were drenched in feelings of guilt; it is as if we felt responsible for the presence of children in the streets. We are responsible as well; it is evident, since we have not had the courage necessary to fight so that such things will not happen. However, we must not fall for purely paternalistic solutions. We would have to study this issue seriously.

I believe that the best one can do is not to fall for what might be called pedagogical optimism, according to which education can accomplish it all, and not to fall for pedagogical pessimism; starting in the eighties and nineties, I believe there has been a search, on a world level, for a more critical, more practical comprehension of educational practice, in which the difficulties and possibilities of education are bared.

GENERATIVE WORD AND CONSTRUCTIVISM

I believe there is a certain freedom, and there are certain misapprehensions. In Brazil, for example, there are those who say—and today it is said less and less—that, after Emília Ferreiro, Paulo Freire *is finished*. I find, first of all, that this statement is lacking on a scientific and philosophical basis. No one *is finished*; everyone is still being. Thus, that is an incompetent observation. I even feel sorry for whoever makes it. I think it is incorrect. Emília Ferreiro is, without a doubt, one of the major contemporary investigators in the field of psycholinguistics. There is no doubt about that. I remember that in a conversation we had in São Paulo, and later, recently in the United States, she said to me, "Paulo, one of the great difficulties we have is how to face the making of research into myth. I mean, deep down, I am a researcher...." Sometimes, people intend for her to be different from something that she is undeniably different from. But I would actually say that Emília lacks one thing—today she is getting closer—that I do not have to spare, as I have exactly in the right proportion, which is an understanding of the *politicalness* of language education. I mean, my pedagogical concern never seems neutral; it never shows up in *itself*. Education is always a political moment.

Now, secondly, among the principles that I was discussing, thirty or forty years ago, was this fundamental respect, which Emília refers to as well—and would have to refer to—this respect that school in general and the educators in particular must have for cultural conditions, for the learner's own cultural identity. I wrote a paper, in the fifties, that my current wife, Nita, who is a historian of education, considers, let us say, fundamental, as one that announced what was yet to come—if I had died, of course, it would not have come, but since I did not die, it came—where I had the cooperation of a team from Pernambuco that participated in the National Conference of Adult Education, in the fifties. The paper has been discussed here and was titled "Educação nos mocambos." It is a three-page paper where I announced, in short, not only literacy education, but a certain fundamental understanding that shows up later, more broadly, in *Pedagogy of the Oppressed*. It is also interesting to observe that that paper on education in the "mocambos" [very poor communities] is fully loaded with my experience at Sesi—it had to be.

Well, it used to be said, then, that I spoke about the generative word while it could not be generative, not the word; it had to be the sentence.... Of course, when I spoke, back in the fifties, in the forties, about generative word, someone who lived in those days and saw any such type of experiment will remember that we started out from a linguistic discourse, that of the learner's language, and not that of the educator's—also one of the fundamental principles of constructivism. Precisely for that reason, then, what needed to be done, according to what I proposed, was a survey on what I called "the learners' minimal vocabulary universe." From that universe, we would select words with which we would go into our experiment. In other words, in fact, what I proposed was an analysis of popular discourse, and later, during the analysis, the apprehension of certain words that were key—within the discourse, not in themselves—so that, with them, in the process of synthesis, we could arrive once more at the global discourse. There is nothing that goes against constructivism in that; on the contrary, that is how human thought operates.

I believe constructivism is a theory of an individual who has a method, who has a technique, who makes use of techniques, of methods. Constructivism is a conception of educational practice—and political as well, albeit that not all constructivists are as political as I am. I cannot be an educator without being political. That does not mean, necessarily, that in order to be an educator one must belong to political party A, B, C, or D. That is not what I am saying. I am referring to being political.

Anyway, what was I proposing then? I proposed that there should be an X period, which at the time we would even admit, of three discussion sessions, with codifications, as I called them, that were done by the great Brazilian artist, from Pernambuco, Francisco Brennand. I had a conversation, set up by Ariano Suassuna, at his house, with a group of artists, Brennand among them, when I spoke about what seemed to me fundamental in order to begin the literacy process, discussion with the literacy learners—an initial discussion, nothing too profound, but a discussion toward understanding the cultural phenomenon. They asked me why it is important to me to put a debate about culture to the literacy learner. I told them the following: the moment you discuss, with groups of literacy learners, what culture is, while human creation and production, deep down, you are making culture, to the extent that you, not simply as a spectator of the world, but as someone who intervenes, who is capable of intervention in the world, are able to change the world. That is the mark of men and women. We become able, while intervening in the world, to do something more than adapting to the world. Culture is the result of the intervention by men and women on a world that they have not created. Therefore, the Beethoven symphony is every bit as much culture as is *Vitalino's ceramic figure*, as is what Tchaikovsky composed, as is this microphone right here in front of me culture, while also a technological expression.

In other words, in reality, what I wanted was to provoke the common man and woman into discovering themselves as competent to make culture as well, even if illiterate. *Why* do that, *what for?* The moment it became possible for literacy learners—and I proved that—to realize that by digging up the ground, finding water, and building a well they are making culture, the moment they discovered that they could change the world and nature that they did not create, then, why would it not be possible to change the world of culture, which is the world of politics, that they make, or that is made upon them?

This is the point at which, for example, I no longer have anything to do with Emília. I mean, Emília's concerns will never lead her to discussing this. What Emília has always done, and continues to do, is research on language production. And that is an extraordinary contribution! My concern was another; it did not escape this moment, but it surpassed this moment. What I wanted was to combat the fatalist ideology according to which God or destiny is responsible for the terrible life of the exploited and the dominated. What I wanted was for the exploited rural worker to realize, finally, that it is not God, or destiny, or fate that can explain the state of destitution in which he or she lives, but rather that it is the social relations of production that can explain his or her life. It was so that they could notice scientific instrumentality, which was this: If I can change a world I did not create, why is it that I do not change the world I make? Why do I not vote differently? Why do I not think differently? Why do I not fight differently?

That was my concern. To make literate, to me, is to do that! Literacy education that stops at *ba-be-bi-bo-bu*.... Well, I would not say it is completely worthless.... Indeed, I believe it would be unfair to say that literacy that stops at *ba-be-bi-bo-bu* is completely worthless. Even that is worth something. After all, it is possible that, after an initial mechanical moment of *ba-be-bi-bo-bu*, the guy might have a flash, and that the educator who is still in the previous phase, that magical, naïve one, of literacy might later discover that the most important thing is changing the world, not just doing the *ba-be-bi-bo-bu*. In other words, the *ba-be-bi-bo-bu* stuff only makes sense when it works toward the radical changing of the world. It is here that I make myself a better man and not when I adapt. It is not by adapting to destitution that I make myself a man, in the plentiful sense of the word, but rather, it is by fighting against destitution, maybe even dying in destitution, but having fought against it! That is it!

You are not obligated to think as I do, but you are obligated to respect me. I respect the individual who seriously tells me, "Paulo, I must confess to you that I, not out of shamelessness, do prefer to accommodate." I pray for that individual, and I feel sorry for him or her, but I cannot hate him or her. After all, I am a democratic person! That is, I grew up learning that it is really in difference that we learn more. I do not learn within equality. If the guy is just like me, thinks like me, does everything like me, likes pork just as I do.... No! He must also like something different. I am all for difference!

But what I really wanted was to say to the rural worker, "Look, you have every right to later discuss this with me; you have every right to say that indeed it is our heavenly Father that wants you to be this way. Now, I have the right and the duty to say that it is not so." God, at the height of paternity, the height of fraternity, at the height of wisdom, of competence, in the highest virtue, cannot discriminate against anyone! Who has ever heard of God's allowing Paulo Freire's children to study, to play Beethoven on the guitar, and allowing the children of others to go hungry? Or that he might do it to test and see if the individual loves him. Who has ever heard of this quality in God? This type of God should not exist! What is necessary is to respect the guy who believes in that kind of god. My duty as a pedagogue, as a political person, is, therefore, that of instrumentalizing. You can accept or not the instrument I am offering, but you must know that this is not true! If you should insist, that is your problem. It is not up to me to arrest you; it is not up to me to kill you; it is not up to me to fire you on account of your believing that, in fact, God is testing you, to see if you love him, and allowing you to not eat. I don't think it is like that.

So that is my concern. Note that the first literacy moment I proposed was exactly that, one of discussion around the cultural phenomenon, so that, starting from a critical understanding of what culture is, they could realize that history is not determination: History is possibility. I mean, the future is not pregiven; the future is not inexorable. The future is problematic. It is up to me, stuck in *futurity* and in *presentification,* to work this future that is coming, that shall come. And that future that shall come is the possibility, or not, to face the dream I have for the world today. What is my dream for the world? It is that of a society less ugly than this one, a society where men and women can love with more ease. My dream for the world is one where there are not thirty-three million Brazilians dying from hunger ... while political scientists keep saying, "That is indeed what reality is...." No, that is not what reality is! Reality is being so because it is in the interest of certain powerful minorities that it remains so! It is necessary to say that this is not true!

In other words, as a literacy educator, what I wanted, in reality—and I never made a secret of that, when I was arrested, here, when they stuck me in a six-by-two cell, about my size (I couldn't even turn because the walls were rough, made of cement)—when they stuck me in such a place, I never abdicated what I thought; I never renounced it. In fact, I would actually laugh.... One day I said to myself, leaning on the wall, God knows how, "Not even Ariano Suassuna, nor any of my friends, could fit in this cell, except for Paulo Rosas." ... Sometimes I, myself, thought it was funny.... That is why, I think, I did not die. It was necessary to create humor to be able to withstand that!

Well, then, I remain, today, the same way. That is, I think, on the contrary, that today I am more radical than when I was at Sesi. But, first, it is necessary to know what radical means. Being radical is not taking to the streets shooting.... No, that is not radicalism; that is insanity, irresponsible lunacy! I am not an irresponsible lunatic. Now, I say that I am radical in the sense of what Marx talked about, of radicalness. He used to say, more or less, this: to me, nothing pertaining to men and women goes unnoticed. I mean, being radical is going to the root of things. The root of things is human interest. It is in that sense that I am radical. But sectarian, myopic, never, not in any way! I respect difference; I respect the right an individual has to be different.

When we proposed that discussion about culture, Brennand painted eight or ten paintings, with very beautiful images, that we turned into slides. In our debates about what we called decodification, which was, in fact, a reading of the world in the representation of the code that I had proposed, evidently, therefore, what came out were not generative words; what came out were sentences, the rural worker's entire discourse. It was from that discourse that I picked up on half a dozen, ten, twelve fundamental words that were then placed at the center of a different debate, so that it could be brought back to the global discourse again.

In other words, it was, in the end, a movement of analysis, of synthesis. There are many people, whom

we also need to respect, but who are intellectually irresponsible, not mattering whether they have been to
university or not. The fact is that they may not have
learned a great deal about the world and think they
have become geniuses, so they go around making ri-
diculous statements. Myself, as a university professor,
I am very demanding and rigorous with respect to the
rights my students have to criticize. However, when
one of them, say in a seminar, criticizes any teacher, I
request a profound explanation as to his or her criticism. I mean, don't even try to give that business of,
"Oh, such and such teacher said some nonsense...."
I ask, first, what is nonsense? What characterizes an
instance of nonsense? What is a nonsensical discourse?
If one cannot explain such things, one is forbidden
from saying them. It can't be like that; one must as-
sume responsibility.

But in a debate aiming to arrive at picking up on, at
comprehending what culture is, a whole discourse came
out, in all its orality, an entire oral comprehension of the
world. Let us say that the word used the first time was
"brick." The codification presented was a man working
at a construction site in Brasília with a brick. And when
we discussed, once again, the generative word *brick*, it
never showed up by itself—*brick*—it always showed up
as it did and as it would again, in sentences, inside a
global discourse. But in the analysis of that global discourse, we picked up on the word after it had come out
in various discourses where it had its meaning. At that
point, we started to analyze the word not grammatically,
but textually, syllabically.

Well, in reality, even if I had not mentioned it as explicitly, I was as demanding on the sentence as on the word. I was as demanding on the sentence as Emília is. What is not possible, however, to Emília and to myself is to escape knowing the word and knowing the analysis of the word. I said, back then already, that literacy education is an act of creation. What is that, then? It means that the literacy learner becomes literate with the help of the literacy educator, but the educator is not the one who puts literacy together for the learner. The literacy learner has to be the subject of the production of his or her writing, just as he or she is the subject of the production of his or her orality.

I think the best one can do today is what BB-Educar[2] does. I would even suggest that you get in touch with BB-Educar because you might develop some very interesting cooperation agreements. BB-Educar, today, carries out work on a Brazil scale. I do not want to mention the number of culture circles that they have today in Brazil to avoid making any mistake, but there are a great many literacy learners in Brazil today following Paulo Freire. Now, what do they do? They do Paulo Freire and Emília Ferreiro. In other words, they are realists; they did not kill me, nor did they do away with Emília; they discovered that both are needed. So I believe that is what needs to be done.

But, dear friends, when I was invited to come here, I said, "At a given point of the conversation I'll end it." That was something else I wanted to tell you I have learned since my time spent here at Sesi. It was this thing I find fantastic, which is a taste for freedom, without ever allowing freedom to deform itself into permissiveness. I mean the freedom that assumes itself as limited, that knows.... I just would not say "that knows its place" because this is a very reactionary and prejudiced phrase. But I have learned that freedom is something wonderful, and that we must use it. I hear that everywhere in the world.

Well, when that given moment comes, I say, "My friends, if we were to continue here now chatting while having a beer, I might actually go for it. But, since that is not the case, and this is a more serious conversation meant to lead us to reflection, I have gotten tired." Not long ago I visited a friend of mine, who was also a superintendent of this house, António Carvalho, who is a little bit older than I am. When I got out of the car, he said, "Paulo, you seem quite older than I am." I said, "I agree." Later, while we were talking, he said, "Paulo, this old-age business is for real." But one of the things that is for real in me today is this, a certain tiredness when it comes to reflection. While I am speaking, I analyze myself a lot. It is an exercise, and a difficult one, but I have managed to experiment with transforming my discourse, just as I am speaking, into a critical object of my reflection. That is how I realize myself in contradiction, or not, at times.

Let me tell you that I was very happy to come back here. I have enjoyed this meeting greatly. I wish to sincerely thank Sesi's superintendent, António Carlos Brito Maciel. I think you hit it right.... You hit it right not because I had something mysterious to say; you were right in accepting the affective need I had for coming here. I thank you enormously for that.

I leave my warm embrace for all of you. And—who knows?—I'll see you in another opportunity.

ENDNOTES

1. Acronym for Movimento de Cultura Popular, created in Recife, on May 13, 1960, by Miguel Arraes, then mayor of the Pernambucan capital. It was in this movement that Paulo carried out the first experiment in the application of what would later be known as "the Paulo Freire method." Paulo Freire was a member of MCP's governing council (Conselho de Direção do MCP), which was extinguished, like other political-educational movements, by the military government soon after the coup of March 1964.

2. Translator's Note: BB-Educar is a literacy education program for young people and adults managed by the Banco do Brasil Foundation. Information in Portuguese about the program can be found at http://www.bb.com.br/appbb/portal/bb/cdn/educ/BBEducar.jsp.

INDEX

✥